We Fought on D-Day

Ulstermen in Normandy – in their own words

MARK SCOTT

COLOURPOINT

Published 2024 by Colourpoint Books
an imprint of Colourpoint Creative Ltd
Colourpoint House, Jubilee Business Park
21 Jubilee Road, Newtownards, BT23 4YH
Tel: 028 9182 0505   E-mail: sales@colourpoint.co.uk   Web: www.colourpointbooks.com

First Edition
First Impression

Text © Mark Scott, 2024
Illustrations © Various, as acknowledged in captions

A catalogue record for this book is available from the British Library.

Designed by April Sky Design, Newtownards
Tel: 028 9182 7195   Web: www.aprilsky.co.uk

Printed by GPS Colour Graphics Ltd, Belfast

ISBN 978-1-78073-387-6

Front cover: Rifleman Edmund James Whitehorn, killed in action on 6th June 1944.
(Whitehorn/Fuller family) and church and church tower, Ranville War cemetery, Ranville,
Normandy. *(Author's own)*
Rear Cover: Top (l-r): Hamilton Lawrence, James Bowden, Richard Keegan, Stanley Burrows.
Bottom (l-r) Bill McConnell, Sam Lowry, Martin Vance, Robert Loughlin.
(All courtesy of DoubleBand Films)

About the author: Mark Scott is a military historical researcher and the author of two previous
non-fiction publications *The Man Who Shot The Great War* and *Among The Kings – The
Unknown Warrior, An untold story*. He has worked as a volunteer researcher with the Royal
Ulster Rifles Museum in Belfast and as a research consultant for the DoubleBand Films'
documentary 'The Man Who Shot The Great War', research which led to his first publication.
Mark applies an investigative approach which is apparent in this latest work. He previously
taught photography at Queen's University in Belfast and has used vintage period Leica
photographic equipment to give an authentic feel to the photography in this publication.

Contents

The author and publisher are very grateful to the following organisations for their vital support, which made the publication of this book possible.

KINDLY SUPPORTED BY

NORTHERN IRELAND WAR MEMORIAL MUSEUM

ACCREDITED MUSEUM

ROYAL ULSTER RIFLES MUSEUM

QUIS SEPARABIT

DOUBLEBAND FILMS

Foreword

Colonel (Retired) Don Bigger,
Chairman of the Trustees,
Northern Ireland War Memorial
February 2024

As Chairman of the Trustees of the Northern Ireland War Memorial (NIWM) I was both honoured and humbled when Mark Scott asked me to write the foreword to this splendid book. The NIWM was delighted to provide financial support to this project as it sits firmly within our mission to tell the story of Northern Ireland's role in the Second World War, and what a story to be told. I wonder how many Ulster folk know that both battalions of the Royal Ulster Rifles served in the Normandy campaign (the first battalion as part of the 6th Airlanding Brigade, arriving in Normandy on the evening of the 6th June 1944 by glider, the second battalion landing in the second wave on SWORD beach from 1030 hrs onwards on D-Day) or that 591 (Antrim) Parachute Field Company Royal Engineers landed by parachute and glider to support the British 6th Airborne Division on the 6th June 1944?

Indeed, as the Corps Historian of the Royal Engineers, a proud Ulsterman with over thirty years' service in the Sappers, a soldier historian and a Normandy Battlefield Tour Guide it has been an absolute pleasure to be involved with this project. Much of the literature on the military history of Ulster in the Second World War focuses on the home front or the Italian Campaign

and not Western Europe; this book goes some way to redress that balance.

At its heart this books tells the proud story of Ulster's involvement in D-Day, and the subsequent Normandy Campaign, through the eyes of the young men who fought in France. The book is deliberately focused on the ordinary soldier's story, and it gives a 'ground truth' version from the slit trench and does not shy away from the realities of war. There is no 'hyperbole' in their words, their deeds are told in a very matter of fact, self-effacing and in many cases amusing manner. We have much to be thankful for from this 'generation of generations.'

That I found all of the book fascinating and at that same time humbling is an understatement. I have used many of the accounts on my Normandy tours and would highlight Bill McConnell's poignant memories of the German sniper he shot and killed in Ranville or of Jimmy Bowden's exploits with the Sappers on D-Day. These are but two of a myriad of fascinating accounts.

The author deals with the sensitive topic of those members of the 2nd Battalion of the Royal Ulster Rifles who were killed (as prisoners of war?) in the fighting with elements of the 12th SS Division 'Hitler Jugend' on the 7th June 1944 in Cambes Wood. He makes a very strong case for a potential war crime – I will let the reader make up their own mind.

It was my privilege to be present at the evening Memorial Service for Rifleman Jim Whitehorn held on the 16th September 2023 at the British Memorial at Ver-sur-Mer just above GOLD Beach. Mark's detail on this event in Chapter 1, The First Rifleman, is both sensitive and compelling. It is a story of sacrifice and in many ways the futility of war and yet a families' mission to remember one who had served on this 'Day of all Days' and made the supreme sacrifice. I defy the reader not to be moved by these events.

Throughout the book all the veterans feel that the exploits of their units have not been remembered enough, nor properly told.

They do not regard themselves as heroes just as ordinary men, who went to war and did their job. In particular they all feel it is of critical importance to remember their mates that did not come home. This book fulfils their wishes. I commend it to you all.

WE WILL REMEMBER THEM

Note: Surnames appearing in the book have been included in capital letters when first mentioned in the various testimonies, or in a report, to assist the reader in connecting events to those involved.

1

The First Rifleman

Ver-Sur-Mer, Normandy
16th September 2023, 18.00hrs

The summer was drawing towards an inevitable end. Rays from the sun, hovering just above a reflecting sea, radiated a soft warmth as golden light fell upon the faces of those gathered on the French hillside overlooking Ver-Sur-Mer. The group, numbering upwards of one hundred assembled; all people who wished to pay their respects to support and comfort a daughter and a family; a person who none of those gathered actually knew, stood in silence around the newly built memorial to those who gave their lives in the fight for the liberation of Europe. A sharp verbal order broke the silence and the pipes and drums of the band of the Police Service of Northern Ireland entered the arena formed by those waiting to the stirring notes of 'Sapper Jack Hassin'. The band marched for a hundred yards wearing their rifle green serge and The Stuart – Prince Charles Edward Modern Tartan with the pendant of the Police Service of Northern Ireland alongside that of the Royal Ulster Constabulary fluttering from the drones of the lead pipers' instruments. The band divided into two single files and lined the walls of the memorial before coming to a halt and turning outwards facing the solemn waiting audience dressed in military uniforms, suits or dark green blazers adorned with medals glinting in the golden evening sunlight.

The Padre began his oration, explaining to all why they were there and leading in prayer to honour the sacrifice made by the fallen, the names of whom were inscribed on the stone of the memorial surrounding everyone gathered on the French hillside. On this occasion, one name was remembered above all others. As a silence descended a lady stepped forward, a mother flanked and supported by two of her sons. She walked towards the memorial wall with an air of uncertainty. An officer stepped forward and handed her a wreath made of red poppies surrounding the insignia of the Royal Ulster Rifles with the name and rank of her father embossed across the center panel and she walked the few steps towards the memorial wall. She stood for a moment in thought before placing the wreath at the foot of the memorial, stepping back bowing her head respectfully for a few seconds then looking back upwards to the name on the wall with a single tear tracing down her cheek. All looked on with a quiet dignity until the silence was broken by the sound of a lone piper, accompanied by a bugler, in perfect harmony filled the air with the stirring notes of the Evening Hymn which merged seamlessly to the bugler's solo rendition of 'Sunset'. As the drones and bugle fell silent Doreen turned and walked towards the crowd gathered along with her family, their heads high. They were among friends she hadn't known, all there to pay their respects. The musicians of The Pipes and Drums marched back into formation and led the way from the monument. Those gathered began to walk away from the memorial wall and talk among themselves. The mood lightened as the band marched off to 'Killaloe', the Regimental March of the Royal Irish Regiment.

On Saturday the 1st June 1944, twelve members of the 2nd Battalion, The Royal Ulster Rifles left their marshalling camp at Warley Barracks in Essex and made their way in lorries to Tilbury Docks on the River Thames, east of London. The men had been separated

from their battalion and restricted to Warley for weeks prior to this, unable to leave and given no explanation as to why they had to remain there. They all knew what was coming but not where, when or how. On arrival at the quayside they were confronted by organised chaos, the scale of which they had never imagined. There, they left their vehicles along with hundreds of others to be loaded on board the waiting ships before returning to Warley. Over the next four days the men attended briefings, waiting in turn in small groups representing regiments, comprising a total of 23,500 men. By 7pm on the 31st May 1944, the loading at Tilbury had been completed. The 23,500 men and 3,375 vehicles had been divided into three convoys of ships, twenty-five in total containing vehicles and drivers forming convoys ETM 1 and ETM 2, along with convoy ETP 1 made up of five more ships containing personnel and their personal equipment. The ships comprising the three convoys, once loaded, sailed the short distance to their final assembly area offshore at Southend in the Thames Estuary. All on board now knew that this was D-1 meaning that the following day would mark the day of the invasion of Europe, D-Day.

The SS *Sambut* was what was known as a 'Liberty Ship,' built in Oregon in the United States in 1943, one of over 2,700 cargo vessels designed and constructed at low cost and high speed to help replace and augment allied shipping which had been lost to German action.[1] The crew of the *Sambut* consisted of 63 men which included two artillery observers and 21 Royal Navy and Army gunners, that were a part of the Defensively Equipped Merchant Ship (DEMS) gunnery crew. In addition, 562 invasion troops, including the 12-man detachment of the 2nd RUR, boarded the ship in small teams extracted from twenty-eight regiments with lorries already packed with ammunition, food, explosives and motor fuel. It was planned that these small teams would land on Sword Beach, near Ouistreham in Normandy on the 7th June

1 Peter Elphick, *Liberty: The Ships That Won The War*, Naval Institute Press, May 2006.

1944, and make their way inland to re-supply their respective regiments and continue the push toward their objectives close to the city of Caen.

The commanding officer of 2nd RUR Headquarters Company had detailed three of his men to join another nine from the battalion to deploy to France on the SS *Sambut*. In a handwritten order, held at the Royal Ulster Rifles Museum in Belfast, Captain M.D.G.C. RYAN had noted the names of the three men and their respective role as follows; Sergeant J McCONVILLE 7010793 Army Catering Corps, Rifleman R WATTERSON 7013045 Motor Transport (MT) driver with a three-ton truck carrying small arms ammunition accompanied by Rifleman E WHITEHORN 7016638 who was an MT fitter. The SS *Sambut* was referred to on Captain Ryan's orders by its code serial number '3211'.[2]

At 06.00hrs on the morning of the 6th June 1944, D-Day, the SS *Sambut* set sail and took up position in convoy ETM 1. The convoy was joined by a Royal Naval escort of four warships as it exited the Thames Estuary and headed south-west into the Dover Strait. The weather was fine and the sea calm, as the convoy made way. The men on board relaxed on deck, checked their equipment, or read from their issued French phrase books. On another ship in the convoy, the SS *Samarovsk*, a military chaplain held a service of worship, during which the men sung hymns and prayed to detract from the job ahead. The scene was documented and recorded by a cameraman from the Army Film and Photographic Unit on board.[3] One of the largest contingents on board the *Sambut* was that of the 92nd (Loyals) Light Anti-Aircraft Regiment (LAA) of the Royal Artillery. The 92nd LAA were part of the 3rd Infantry Division divisional support troops of which the 2nd Royal Ulster Rifles formed a part. Their primary role was to provide anti-aircraft cover for the Division during the Normandy

2 Captain MDGC Ryan, personal papers RUR Museum, Bedford Street, Belfast.
3 I.W.M. Catalogue No. A70 36-5, Film, 'Reinforcements for the Invasion of Normandy', War Office, Army Film and Photographic Unit, Connolly J.R.

landings and the advance inland, as such they were equipped with 40 mm Bofors anti-aircraft guns. These weapons were either towed or mounted onto a Morris C9B commercial lorry chassis. Although the primary use of these guns were in an anti-aircraft role, they were equally effective against ground targets, potentially unleashing high explosive shells at a devastating rate of 120 rounds per minute. A total of 120 men of the 92nd LA were on board the *Sambut* on the morning of the 6th June; for this reason, there are a number of accounts of an incident documenting what transpired to be the biggest single loss of life suffered by the invasion forces that took part in the D-Day 'Operation Neptune' landings.

As midday approached on board the *Sambut* many of the men on board began to assemble in the mess deck waiting for food to be served. Two men from the 92nd LAA later recalled an incident that had almost immediate consequences for all on board.[4] Bill Wills, a 20-year-old driver, remembered that as the *Sambut* was off Dover a Royal Navy escort ship came alongside. An officer on board used a megaphone to instruct the master of the *Sambut* to lower a barrage balloon which had been raised from the deck for protection from enemy aircraft while offshore at Southend. As the convoy passed the cliffs of Dover at the narrowest part of the English Channel the balloon provided a marker against the backdrop of the white cliffs onto which the German coastal guns on the French coast, some 19 miles away could range onto the ships below. Bill's colleague, Bombardier Tom Cribb later recalled the balloon stating, '*It was obviously too high as the Germans could see it against the cliffs*'. Bill later recounted, '*I don't know if the Master had time to comply as shortly after the shells struck. It is very likely the Germans used the balloon to lay their guns.*'

Bill Wills describes the moment, '*Then, just as we passed Dover,*

---

4   Tom McCarthy, *True Loyals: A History of 7th Battalion, The Loyal Regiment (North Lancashire)/92nd (Loyals) Light Anti-Aircraft Regiment, Royal Artillery, 1940-1946*, 2nd ed., Countyvise Editions Ltd., Birkenhead, 2012, republished online.

there was an enormous explosion just before the bridge and a lot of people thought we had been torpedoed. We saw a fire near the bridge. The ship had large fire extinguishers on wheels, but they apparently didn't work. There were quite a lot of further explosions, with lots of nasty bits and pieces flying about. We were told to put our ammunition over the side to stop any further explosions.'

The *Sambut* had been fired upon by a volley of 16-inch shells fired from the German coastal battery at Cap Gris-Nez on the Calais coast. It had been thought that the large naval guns that made up the battery could not traverse quickly enough to be able to harass the shipping that made its way up and down the English Channel at this point. Perhaps the balloon had made ranging the guns onto the convoy easier; in any case the *Sambut* had been struck a fatal blow with two of the four shells fired striking the deck and bridge areas. The incident was witnessed by men of the 182nd Infantry Brigade from an observation post at Dover; they made an entry in their War Diary as follows – *'Convoy moving WEST through STRAITS of DOVER shelled by GERMANS, four shells landing, one ship hit and set on fire.'* The time of this entry was recorded as 12.15hrs.

The details of the incident can be found in the official report made to the War Office Casualty Branch made to the Admiralty.[5] The report gives the time of the shelling as 12.03hrs, off Dover and east of Goodwin Sands in fine, sunny weather with clear visibility.

The official report stated that fire broke out on board immediately, accelerated by the cargo of petrol, diesel and explosives carried by the trucks loaded onto the deck. The Master of the ship, Captain Mark Willis, reported that all those capable of doing so had abandoned the ship by 12.30hrs. He further reported that of the 63 crew on board two were killed, four injured and one missing. Of the 562 invasion troops recorded as being on board a figure of 'approx. 150' were recorded as missing as of 30th November 1944. The death toll was later revised to 136 killed or missing, 130 of

5   The National Archives, WO 361/597 SS *Sambut.*

them were soldiers of the invasion force along with six members of the ship's crew.

The SS *Sambut* was reported to have been sunk later that day by the Royal Navy as its smoldering hulk presented a navigational hazard to the high volume of shipping using the channels cleared for passage and swept for mines. Remarkably, the official film cameraman who had recorded the scenes of men preparing for battle and attending the religious service on board the nearby *Samarovsk* managed to turn his camera towards the stricken *Sambut* and record footage of the ship burning with rescue launches in attendance.[6] The footage can be viewed as a part of the Imperial War Museum archive.

In the weeks and months following the sinking enquiries were made regarding the fate of those on board. Survivors were picked up by a small flotilla of motor launches which arrived at the stricken vessel within minutes of the artillery strike and men were plucked from the sea and eventually brought to Dover Castle for any treatment and to re-group before being eventually sent again to Normandy to rejoin their various units. There was an inevitable delay in communicating details of the various losses to their respective battalions. This administrative delay caused confusion and frustration for loved ones of those involved as men were initially declared 'missing' or 'missing at sea,' sometimes for long periods of time before being declared 'killed in action', a classification that required evidence from a credible witness.

Eleven of the twelve men of the 2nd Royal Ulster Rifles party on board the vessel were recovered alive from the sea and continued to serve with the battalion. One rifleman however was lost in the action; the circumstances of his death and the reporting of the same to his next of kin caused confusion and grief that perpetuated for almost eighty years.

Rifleman Edmund James (Jim) Whitehorn, service number

---

6 I.W.M. Catalogue No. A70 36-5, Film, 'Reinforcements for the Invasion of Normandy', War Office, Army Film and Photographic Unit, Connolly J.R.

7016638 was 24 years old in June ,1944. He was married to Emmie and the couple had a nine-month-old baby girl, Doreen. Jim had trained as a mechanic and from 1942 he had been attached to the battalion Motor Transport (MT) section as a MT fitter. Jim and Emmie came from and lived in Stepney in East London.

It is not clear when Jim's wife Emmie was first notified of Jim's loss. The first official document relating to him dates from 3rd July 1944 when his name was listed in the War Office Casualty Branch return no. 1488, his status at that time was recorded as 'Missing at sea' as a result of action on 6th June 1944. If Emmie had been informed of his loss up to that date, almost a full month from 6th June then that is what she would have been told, that her husband was missing at sea. This bland statement however instilled an element of hope in Emmie's mind. There was a chance that her husband could still have been alive, so many scenarios ran through her thoughts. The report stated that he was missing 'at sea'. Again, by July 1944, Emmie was aware of what had taken place on the Normandy beaches four weeks earlier, had she thought Jim had been separated during the landing at Sword Beach? Or was he in a field hospital maybe suffering from concussion or memory loss and hadn't been identified? Had he been taken prisoner by the Germans? Or any combination of scenarios could have meant that he could have walked back into their house in Stepney and their lives could have continued together. The fact was, Emmie never gave up hope of seeing Jim again and as the weeks passed, she held onto that hope.

On the 1st August 1944, following an enquiry by the War Office Casualty Branch, Jim Whitehorn's name was again added to the ongoing casualty list. On this occasion he was recorded as having been 'killed in action' on the 6th June 1944 'at sea'. On the same day Jim's company commander Captain S. Beavan sent a letter to Emmie from 'the field'.[7] He wrote:

---

7 Whitehorn/Fuller family archive.

Dear Mrs. Whitehorn,

I am writing to you to express my very deep sympathy with you in the loss of your husband. I would explain that I was transport officer of this battalion and your husband worked with me for nearly two years. I shall always recall his cheerfulness and willingness, even under the most trying circumstances.

I was extremely sorry to hear of his death, but I feel sure you would like to know that the hard work he put in on the battalion's vehicles contributed in no small manner to our successful landing. As a fitter he was first class and so far we have not lost one vehicle from breakdowns and a lot of that is due to his efforts.

I hope you will not feel he laid down his life in vain. I know you must be feeling his loss and we of the Transport Platoon sympathise very deeply with you.

With best wishes to you for the future, I remain,

Yours sincerely
S Beavan

On the 1st August 1944, the day he penned his letter to Emmie, Captain Beavan and the men of the 2nd RUR had taken up a rest position at Bieville in Normandy.[8] They had been in action and in constant contact with the enemy since landing on D-Day. It is fair to say that the captain's knowledge of what had happened to Jim Whitehorn was minimal. His letter did not state how Jim lost his life, or even when, let alone where; it gave no further clue to Emmie as to what happened to her husband. Captain Beavan simply did not know.

The first official record of Jim Whitehorn's death appeared in the official 'History of the 2nd Bn. The Royal Ulster Rifles in Northwest Europe 1944-45'.[9] This official volume listed a Roll of Honour of

---

8 The National Archives, WO 171/1384, War Diary, 2nd Royal Ulster Rifles.
9 'The History of the 2nd Bn. The Royal Ulster Rifles in North West Europe 1944-45' ACC 872, Royal Ulster Rifles Museum, Bedford Street, Belfast.

those officers and men who gave their lives between June 6th 1944 and May 8th 1945. In this publication Rifleman E Whitehorn was recorded with an incorrect service number 7016683 instead of 7016638, his date of death was recorded as 12th June 1944 which was possibly the date when the 2nd Battalion were initially notified of his death or, more correctly, the date he was reported missing. In a further published Roll of Honour for the battalion there was an entry in the name of Rifleman F Whitehorn as opposed to E. Again, the service number was 7016683 and the date of death recorded as 12th June 1944.

What we know now is that at some point between the 3rd July and the 1st August 1944, the two dates on which his name appeared on the official casualty lists, his status had been changed from 'missing at sea' to 'killed in action'. Such a change had to have been made as a result of an interview with someone who actually witnessed Jim's death or who saw his body. Unfortunately the details of this report, once confirmed and accepted were weeded from the official record and no longer appear in the official file relating to the incident. It is safe to assume however that the witness to his death had to have been someone who knew him, one of the other eleven Riflemen on board who were part of the Royal Ulster Rifles MT detachment. The witness was most likely one of the two men in his own company who were detailed to be on board that day, either Sergeant J McConville or rifleman R Watterson, of these two, Rifleman Watterson, as an MT driver would have worked more closely with Jim Whitehorn, sergeant McConville being Army Service Corps, attached to the Royal Ulster Rifles. In any case his name does not now appear on the National Archives' report of the sinking of the SS *Sambut*.

In Stepney, East London, Emmie Whitehorn had to come to terms with raising her only daughter Doreen alone. The muddled reporting of Jim's death, compounded by the level of secrecy applied during the buildup to the Normandy invasion and then the initial 'missing' report unfortunately, and understandably,

led her to believe that someday, as she was going about her life, Jim would walk through the door and their lives would continue together from where they left off.

Emmie Whitehorn received an invitation to attend the unveiling of the Bayeux Memorial to The Missing which was built at the site of a war cemetery of the same name in Calvados, Normandy. The unveiling took place on the 5th June 1955. The memorial bears the names of over 1,800 men who were killed during the initial stages of the Normandy campaign and who have no known grave. On that day the memorial was unveiled by the Duke of Gloucester. Emmie declined the invitation to attend, along with numerous subsequent invitations. Until her passing, at 103 years of age in 2012, she never remarried, refused to accept her husband Jim's loss and avoided any conversation about his military service.

One day in the 1970s she was shopping with her daughter Doreen close to where they lived at Stepney. The two ladies went into a hardware shop and on making a purchase the shopkeeper recognised Emmie and began to chat to her. Doreen, not involved in the conversation, continued to browse in the shop and only half listened to the conversation at the counter. It transpired that the shopkeeper had served with Jim Whitehorn and he made some comment to Emmie regarding a ship. Doreen, unaware that the conversation was about her father paid little attention and continued to look around before leaving when her mother had completed the purchase. It was only recently, in 2022, when she was contacted during the research for this publication that Doreen realised the significance of the conversation in the hardware shop. If Emmie had been told new facts, then she did not divulge them to her daughter. Perhaps even then she held on to a hope that Jim might return to her.

As the band marched away from the memorial and the music dimmed, I stole a glance at Doreen, surrounded and supported by her family with the wreaths of poppies at her feet. I wondered at the life her mother had lived and what thoughts had haunted

her in dark unguarded moments when alone, waiting for her beloved Jim to walk back into her life. Jim Whitehorn was spared the horrors and blows that were dealt to his colleagues, the dark incidents which I learned about, the relief of victory and the demons that haunted those who won it for years to follow. He was the first member across both battalions of the Royal Ulster Rifles to be killed in action during D-Day. I hoped deep down that Doreen could feel some warmth in knowing that her father was no longer lost, she knew of his fate and where he lay. I hoped that in her mind he was no longer missing. He had been remembered.

Rifleman Edmund James 'Jim' Whitehorn.
Killed in Action, 6th June 1944 on board the SS *Sambut*.

2

The Airborne Landings

East of the River Orne
Bénouville, Pegasus Bridge

20.00hrs D-Day minus 1

James Henry BOWDEN came from East Belfast, he was born in Central Street and grew up in Roundhill Street. Both streets which are no longer in existence in the city today. James had been a member of the Territorial Army for two years until he was called up for war service in 1939 just before his nineteenth birthday and spent the early years of the war in England serving with the 591 (Antrim) Field Company of The Royal Engineers which was part of the 54th Infantry Division. The 54th Division covered the East Anglia area in an anti-invasion role and would have been responsible for the demolition of bridges and actions to disrupt an enemy invasion landing. In May of 1943 James' unit changed name and role to the 591 (Antrim) Parachute Squadron of the Royal Engineers. He became part of the 6th Airborne Division and trained accordingly, an indication perhaps of things that were to come.

On the 17th February 1944 orders were issued to the 6th Airborne Division to devise a plan to land a parachute brigade along with an airborne anti-tank artillery battery in enemy-occupied Normandy to seize, intact if possible, and hold the bridges which spanned the River Orne and the parallel Caen Canal

at Ranville and Benouville.[1] This plan was part of larger 'Operation Overlord' invasion of Europe with this element designed to deny the defending German forces access to the area west of the Orne where the main seaborne invasion force was to land. Initially the task of seizing the bridges was assigned to the 6th Air-landing Brigade utilising their gliders in preference to a parachute drop assault. It was thought that a substantial concentration of effort combined with the heavier armament that could be carried and landed by glider would be deemed more effective in accomplishing the task and would provide the troops with anti-tank artillery to assist in defending the area east of the Orne against an inevitable German counterattack.

In mid-April 1944 intelligence was received that meant the initial planning had to be changed.[2] Analysis of aerial photography from a Royal Air Force reconnaissance flight across the proposed landing zones indicated that wooden poles, similar in size to telegraph poles, had been erected across open ground effectively obstructing all the proposed glider landing areas. It was later discovered that the German defending forces had attached Tellermines, anti-tank mines containing five and a half kilos of TNT explosive, to the defensive poles. These defensive poles were soon given the nick-name 'Rommel's Asparagus' after their appearance and the German Field Marshal who directed that they were to be erected as part of his Atlantic Wall defences.

It was decided that 5 Parachute Brigade Group (5 Para) would carry out an initial parachute assault in the areas of the proposed landing zones to clear the fields of the defensive poles, neutralise the explosive Tellermines and facilitate the safe landing of the main glider force. 5 Para Brigade was commanded by Brigadier Nigel POETT. He had assembled and trained his men from scratch since May 1943. By June 1944 he had at his disposal four

---

1 The National Archives, '6 Airborne Division Report on Operations in Normandy 6 June to 27 August 1944' CAB 106/970.
2 Ibid.

anti-tank batteries of the Royal Artillery, a glider-borne company of the 2nd Battalion of the Oxford and Buckinghamshire Light Infantry, 286 (Airborne) Field Park Company Royal Engineers, 225 (Parachute) Field Ambulance of the Royal Army Medical Corps and the 591 (Antrim) Parachute Squadron of the Royal Engineers, Jimmy Bowden's unit.[3] Brigadier Poett's specific objectives were as follows:

(i) With a 'Coup de Main' force of gliderborne troops seize the crossings over the River Orne and Canal at Benouville and Ranville.

(ii) Secure and hold the area Benouville – Ranville – Le Bas de Ranville.

(iii) Capture and neutralise the artillery battery at grid 107765, the 'Merville' battery.

(iv) Clear the landing zones north of Ranville of obstructions to allow 68 gliders to land by two hours before daylight and 146 gliders by the evening of D-Day. The Brigade was also responsible for the protection of the landing zone on which the larger glider element was to land.

On Monday the 5th June 1944, with his objectives outlined, Jimmy Bowden from East Belfast found himself at the sharp end of the biggest invasion in the history of mankind.

James BOWDEN:

'On the 5th of June 1944 we had been in the concentration camp for 10 days, we weren't allowed out, studying the maps and models. On that day we were preparing, getting our kit bags prepared with what we needed. We had laid down how many rounds of ammunition, grenades, our rations – forty-eight-hour rations – and so forth. We were taking off at 11 o'clock at night on the 5th of June so it was suggested that we have a couple of hours rest then have our meal at about 8 o'clock and at 9 o'clock we set off. We were

---

3 Ibid.

at Harwell, and they brought us in trucks and took us out to Gloucestershire to an airfield at Fairford. It took us quite a while going there by truck and it was funny going through some of the villages, people seeing us and saying 'there's lads heading out on exercise' but we were actually on our way to France, kids waving at us just before dark.

The atmosphere in the camp was a question of getting things right and studying. Everyone was keen to know exactly what we were going to do. We had been preparing for months and months. The feeling I would say was tense, some of the younger ones, I mean I was 23 but some of the younger ones of about 18 or 19, who I would say shouldn't have been there, they were too tense and a bit scared you know, the rest of us who had been in the army for some time were scared, yes, but not too scared as we had to think about what we were doing and make sure we did it right. As regards the jumping we were all familiar, we had all done about 18 or 19 jumps, so it wasn't that we were so worked up about what we were doing we hadn't time to feel scared. We had been training for months and months and we just hadn't time to be scared.

The day before we were told we could write one letter home to say you were going and it won't be posted until after you had gone to let your people know that you were involved in the Normandy landings you see. I just wrote to my mother and said that the chances are that we might not come back. You know, we felt that there was a good chance of being killed. Knowing the position of the troops on the Atlantic Wall and knowing we were landing; you know you could land in amongst them and be shot right away. I remember writing it, but it was my mother I was worried about, it wasn't about myself. I was more or less resigned that I might not come out of it and many of us were the same. They told us we were going to have casualties and they reckoned that on the landing, the whole of the landing, we would have 25,000 casualties on the day. Just on the

beaches. These are men just going there to be killed and that's it. I didn't have time to feel too scared.

The objective was, we landed together close to wood. We were to find that as quickly as we could then work ourselves into teams, several teams to blow up poles, to make a runway for the gliders coming in. It was imperative that we got this done before 3am. The General had said he was coming in at 3 o'clock no matter what so we had to get those poles down, not out of the way necessarily, but down. It was very important to get the anti-tank guns in and it was imperative that the bridges were held.'

Jimmy Bowden's recollections of the detail of his mission give us a unique insight into his perception of the effects of the intelligence war that was playing out behind the scenes. It became apparent to the command that Rommel had received intelligence that a gliderborne assault on his Atlantic Wall defences was likely, hence his installation of the 'Rommel's asparagus' defensive poles. British intelligence subsequently discovered their existence, and a revised plan was implemented, the details of which impacted on Jimmy's training, the key elements of which were fine-tuned and thoroughly practiced out prior to the landings.

James BOWDEN:
'Rommel had said that all these fields were ideal for gliders. "They [the British] have an Airborne Division being formed at the moment and bringing in gliders." They started off with telegraph poles and dug down and planted them there all over the fields right around Ranville and all that area. We saw those from aerial photographs and studied them. They reckoned they were mostly telegraph poles and later there was just saplings as they were running out of telegraph poles. We practiced, we made these charges with bicycle tubes filled with plastic explosives and then got gun cotton stuck in the end and then a detonator and safety fuse and

that was it, charge ready. We blew up poles and practiced. The gliders were made up from very light material, if the poles hadn't been taken away the gliders would have crashed and splintered.'

By 23.00hrs on the evening of the 5th June 1944 at Fairford Airfield, Jimmy had completed his preparations. He was carrying so much equipment that he had to be helped onto the transport plane and once the door was closed and secured behind him his D-Day had begun, he was on his way to enemy-occupied France.

James BOWDEN:
'So, we set off at about 11 o'clock and we circled round and round until we could get going in one group. Each plane had their own navigator, not like the Americans. The Americans had one navigator for a whole squadron of planes, they went in threes and the plane in front had a navigator, the two planes either side just followed on and the other planes just followed them, but we had our own navigator. We got word from the pilot that we were heading to France. We crossed the Channel, and we could see the beaches somewhere around Cabourg, it wasn't actually as far down as Ranville or the bridges, we could see the beaches and as we saw the beaches anti-aircraft fire came up. We started taking evasive action, swinging around, but that was only for about a minute or two. When we were clear of that he (the pilot) said, "Five minutes to go". Ready, red light on, green light goes, and that was it.'

Jimmy, at that moment, encountered a problem that was to trouble the men making the seaborne landings later that day; that of how to dispose of his bicycle. It had been directed that the invasion troops carry bicycles along with their normal equipment, the idea being that once the initial landings were made the men could move quickly by bike towards the main objective which

ultimately was the city of Caen. Deploying infantry by bicycle had been used during the Great War with whole battalions formed and trained as Cyclist Corps but from the attitude and actions of the men lumbered with this additional piece of kit it is fair to say that by the 6th June 1944 the idea and tactic had had its day.

James BOWDEN:

'My troop commander, Fergie Semple was jumper number one. He was told, as we had some bicycles and things, tools, and things, he was told to throw those out of the plane first, particularly the folding bicycles, get them out. He said to me to hold onto him while he was doing it. So, he was leaning over the hole and throwing these bikes out when we got the word to go. As soon as we got the word to go, he went out and I was still holding on to him, so I really fell out after him. Then I started to get my kit bag loose, there was a sort of a pin to click away and sort of pay it out. What happened then was as I was paying out the rope, I didn't appreciate the weight, it was 70 pounds, I just ran it through my hands and the next thing I felt was that it was gone. I landed ok, I mean we were jumping at about five or six hundred feet, so it was only a matter of about eleven or twelve seconds at the most. I was down on the ground with nothing except a knife, a fighting knife and my ammunition but I had no rifle, no small kit, no nothing.'

Jimmy at this point had to use his own initiative. He had modestly described parachute deployment as being simply a means of transport into battle but at this point he realised that in essence, by nature, a paratrooper fought a battle from the starting position of being surrounded by the enemy. Jimmy, regardless of how, like many veterans, he later in a modest way described his role during D-Day, had to survive on wits and draw on his training.

James BOWDEN:

'I was on my own. But I mean, every time you jumped you were on your own. Even doing practice jumps you were on your own till you met up with your people, what was called a 'stick'. But that was daylight, daylight was different you see. You could see around you and see people coming behind you and so on. But then, (on D-Day) I couldn't see a thing. When I landed, I landed on my own, I couldn't see a thing in the dark, I didn't know where the hell I was. It was important that we had got to the right place. There was a Squadron Leader, he took the planes himself and he briefed us beforehand and he said he was quite confident that he would get us there. That Squadron Leader gave me confidence that he knew what he was doing and where he was going, he was very experienced. You were hoping that you weren't going to be on your own very long, just hoping.

I was scared when I lost my equipment and I had to search around amongst, I don't know what it was, whether it was corn or wheat or what, so I found another kit bag with a rifle and everything else because everyone had the same thing a small haversack, spare shirt, eating tools you know. Of course, I had my own personal grenades and explosives, to destroy the poles we all had about three or four charges with us. I had them around my neck. I decided that I've got to find out where I am, so I saw a hedge and I went over and knelt down beside the hedge to see if there was anybody on the road. I heard some feet, quite a few people came along then I heard the voices, they were English. I got out onto the road, who are you? 7th battalion they said, they were going to the Bridges, Pegasus Bridge, it had been captured but they needed men to defend it and that was their job. I said I'll go along with you. I knew where they were going but I wasn't going to the bridges so I went down this road and low and behold there was this signpost, I couldn't believe it 'Benouville

6 km'. I was told by the French later that the Germans had left all of the signposts up so that they could find their way around. Once I saw that, from my memory of the maps, I knew exactly where I was.

Just as I was about to go across a field there was a lad beside me, it was one of our lieutenants, Lieutenant James, he was about 21 or 22. Although our faces were blackened, I still recognised him, and he recognised me. He said, 'Do you know where we are?' and I said 'Yes, the wood is over there' [the rendezvous]. So we made it to the rendezvous ok. For me it just happened that I met this lieutenant, and he knew and I knew where we were going. It was just luck or training I suppose, you had to concentrate on what you were doing.'

Once Jimmy had made his way to the landing zone areas he linked up with the other engineers of his unit and set about his allotted tack of destroying the poles and neutralising any mines attached to them. He went about his work generally unhindered, pausing briefly when machine-gun fire was heard overhead.

James BOWDEN:
'We were going along in a line blowing them up (the poles) and suddenly, from the right machine-gun fire went over our heads. We all went down and the troop captain, he edged forward, and he shouted a password, the password was 'V', and the reply was 'Victory'. 'V' for victory you know. They were English fellows and he shouted, 'What the hell are you firing at?' they replied, 'There was a truck going down the road there'. They saw this truck and it couldn't have been one of ours as they hadn't landed on the beaches yet so it must have been the Germans, that's what they were firing at, so that was ok. We just carried on then and finished what we had to do. The troop captain then said, 'that's enough' as it was getting near 3 o'clock and they would be coming in, and they did.'

The 591 (Antrim) Squadron had deployed by air in three 'Troops'. One of them, 2 Troop, was to assist in the assault of the Merville gun battery, codenamed Point Hillman north of Ranville. This artillery installation was deemed to be a serious threat to the proposed beach landings and had to be neutralised prior to the main assault. The battery at Merville was taken in heroic fashion by a drastically depleted assault force led by ex-Royal Ulster Rifles Colonel Terence OTWAY. The engineers of 2 Troop landed off target and could not join his assault.

The men of 1 and 3 Troop, which included Jimmy Bowden, on landing at 1.00am numbered just 12 men under Lieutenant James, the officer who Jim had joined after landing alone. It had been planned that they clear four landing strips, two for Horsa gliders and two for the larger Hamilcar gliders. By 2.15am they had succeeded in clearing the two Horsa strips when they were joined by the rest of their party along with Captain Semple who had jumped first from Jimmy's plane.

After 3.00am the gliders began to land, arriving from all directions, some landing at the same time from opposite directions and many crashing into the 'Rommel's Asparagus' poles on fields that had not been cleared. Remarkably very few casualties were recorded.

By 5.00am the engineers of 591 (Antrim) Squadron had completed the task of clearing the landing zones and began to dig in around the Divisional Headquarters position which had been established at Bas de Ranville. In advance of German counter attacks, they were tasked with laying a minefield forward of the positions held at Ranville.

Jimmy Bowden could recall hearing the Royal Naval batteries off the Normandy coast open up with covering fire which indicated to him that the seaborne invasion landings were in full swing. He took time to reflect on his own position.

James BOWDEN:

'Well, we knew that they were going to start at about 4 o'clock and we were told that once they were starting to land that the cruisers would open up with their guns. Sure enough when we broke cover at daylight we had these big shells over our heads, you could hear them a mile away you know. Eight-inch guns, off the beaches they were covering. We had lost quite a few. Half a troop in one plane landed miles away and were all taken prisoner. The other plane, where our commanding officer got out, we lost about ten or so, that was about another ten or so. We had quite a few missing on D-Day but we were lucky. I was lucky to get landed in the proper place. I was happy when the main invasion started. If they hadn't started, well we would have been sunk, as there was no way of us getting out right away you see. We were confident, psyched up as regards to what was happening and knowing too that those beach defences were terrific. In fact we used to say, 'God help those lads landing on the beaches', at least we were landing practically unopposed, we were lucky to have joined the paras! Otherwise, we would have been landing on those beaches. They'd all those big guns on the shore firing at you and you were out in the open, at least in the Paras we could get in behind hedges and what not and keep in a bit of cover once we landed.'

21.00hrs D-Day
Landing Zone 'N', Ranville

At 9.00pm that evening the 1st (Airborne) Battalion of the Royal Ulster Rifles landed on the strips of landing zone or 'LZ' N, cleared by 591 Squadron. The 147 gliders carrying the Battalion came in on time just north of the village of Ranville. Jimmy Bowden witnessed them land, an event which left an indelible mark on his memory.

James BOWDEN:

'We were all round the zone where the gliders had landed and we were part of the defence of that zone, the Germans were behind us then. As the gliders were coming in just before dark, the Ulster Rifles, and the others, but not the Devons, the Devons came in by sea, it was the Ox and Bucks and the first battalion of the RUR coming in. As they were landing the Germans opened up with their mortars, you couldn't see the gliders hardly for the explosions and all, and out of all this mess came these men running, shouting, we knew they were Ulster Rifles all right, and they were going into action. I used to admire the Rifles because of the speed they used to go at you know. They were always taught to go at speed. They landed and these fields were being shelled like nobody's business. I don't know what casualties they had as we couldn't see. All I know was that out of all the dust and dirt and all came these fellows running with Jeeps, alongside Jeeps, and carrying their Vickers machine guns. It was like something out of a film. To film that, I'm telling you it would have been brilliant to see the way these fellas were running. The next thing was their machine guns opened up as the Germans had got in behind us. A good job too that they came as they [the Germans] would have been hitting us. They gave them a hell of a welcome, the Germans did, oh aye. That was the evening of D-Day.'

Samuel LOWRY, Bill McCONNELL, Martin VANCE, and Robert LOUGHLIN were members of the 1st (Airborne) Battalion, The Royal Ulster Rifles, who were part of the airborne glider assault that evening. Any one of them could have been among the group of riflemen running into action on landing as described by Jimmy Bowden. The formation and structure of the Airborne Division regiments was described by Sam Lowry, who was a platoon sergeant in June 1944.

Samuel LOWRY:

'I was nearly 18, working in the aircraft factory. A few of my friends had joined up and I came from an army family, four uncles, my father and my grandfather before me had been army. Whether it was the sense of adventure, I know I was supposed to be sleeping as I was working night shift at the aircraft, but lo and behold Sam ended up at the recruiting office one morning and I finished up in Ballymena that day with the paltry sum of three and fourpence, that was for my pay, and I was a soldier. It happened very quickly; I never had a chance to get my breath back really.

In nineteen and forty when I joined up there was what is known as Young Soldiers battalions called the 70th, I joined one of those and served with them until March 1942 when our 1st Battalion who were coming home from India were entering the Airborne Division. They were looking for so-called volunteers, but it wasn't volunteers because my whole company went up. These were all lads, some may have been 16 (years) and their birth certificates got disfigured I don't know, but I estimate that roughly 120 of us went up at that time.

The 1st Battalion at that time was in a brigade that had come home from India consisting of the South Staffs [South Staffordshire Regiment], the Border Regiment and the Ox and Bucks [Oxfordshire and Buckinghamshire Light Infantry]. They all formed the First Airlanding Brigade which were not Paras, they were glider troops. No glider ever carried a parachute. We moved up there to the 1st Battalion, the 1st Battalion at that time was stationed at Highbury. We came back later on to Beauford where we consolidated as a battalion again and part of the Brigade and so we started training as the 1st Airlanding Brigade and devoted most of our training to Airborne tactics.'

Sam followed an intensive airborne training syllabus through 1943 and into 1944. During this period, he and his colleagues

bonded into a cohesive fighting unit. As the months passed and the war raged across the globe the airborne troops knew that they were being trained up and held back from the fighting for a specific purpose, the detail of which remained secret until the final moment.

Sam LOWRY:

'Any sane thinking person training with first class troops realised that an invasion had to take place and if you had been training and training for it there was no way of you missing it. No one was going to miss it. It wasn't eager anticipation; it was just every day was a day nearer and that was it.

It wasn't a feeling of fear, at that time I would say there was a sort of a mystic screen. You trained but yet at the end you couldn't see a positive objective but yet it was there, and you knew it. It's so very very hard to describe the feeling over those years; actually, from forty-two, forty-three and forty-four.

Then we had met people coming back from raids. When the Saint Nazaire Raid was pulled off in forty or forty-one, we were in Plymouth in barracks and we helped to take their wounded ashore, so we weren't green. Also, as young soldiers we had helped to clear the streets in Belfast after the Blitz. We were sort of a way attuned as far as possible to the perils and terrors of war and the obscene spectacles that you are going to see.'

During the final days before the invasion, Sam, still unaware of exactly what lay ahead, was moved along with the other 1st RUR men to a transit camp. Such was the level of secrecy imposed during those final stages of preparation that at the time of his interview, some 60 years later, Sam was still unclear as to where he actually was.

Sam LOWRY:

'I don't know even the name of the aerodrome. I think, I think it was Brize Norton as in those days because that was a big glider place, it could have been but to be frank with you my knowledge around the airfield etcetera was very limited. We were confined mostly to our own tents; the canteen was open and that was that. It was a sort of a miasma. You were walking through it, you were set, you were disciplined. You had to make sure everybody was ready, and everybody was equipped. Bearing in mind that as an airborne troop, the first priority of any army and any soldier will tell you is ammunition. You had to carry more ammunition than the normal soldier going in by sea. That had to be prepared, that had to be checked and grenades had to be primed. Some last-minute drills with some people. That sort of thing.

We went over a map where names had been removed and photographic maps where names had been removed. We were to do a frontal attack at Ranville and if that was successful we were to go on to Longueval and take it. The plan of action was laid down by the Colonel at the 'O Groups' or order groups and passed on to company commanders who in turn passed it on.

You had a rough idea it was going to be on a very large scale, you would have had to have been a donkey, reading press reports, seeing what was going on round you, seeing the various outfits and units coming back and forth to say there was nothing happening on a large scale!

I seem to recall it was early reveille for D-Day itself, it was a scene of hustle, bustle, getting checked up then loading up to the gliders. We took off after our last briefing, our maps were issued and in one particular case escape maps were issued, a lovely little silk one, and off we went. If you were able to look out at the gliders and the trains of gliders, don't forget, the Wellingtons and the Lancasters were the tug planes and if you saw that airfield the tow ropes stretched out ready for the tug plane to take over and

the glider pilot ready to link up, it was very, very impressive. I mean they weren't going off in fours and fives, I don't know if they were going off in hundreds but if you take one glider for a platoon, three companies to a battalion, even six companies, there's six fours, twenty-four, seventy-two… you go into astronomical figures. Going across you could see the sea convoys underneath if you could stand up to look out. You could see the gliders either side of you with their distinctive white stripe markings. All I could see was ships. I was thinking, 'at least there's a load more going over here, we're all right.' That's all I could think of, it looked impressive, there's no two ways about it.'

Martin 'Marty' VANCE had taken a similar route to D-Day as his colleague Sam Lowry. On enlisting at 17 years old he trained initially at Omagh in County Tyrone before joining the 70th Young Soldiers Battalion of the Royal Ulster Rifles then moved on to airborne training with the 1st Battalion. He described a build up of tension once his battalion moved to the transit camp at Brize Norton.

Martin VANCE:
'We were at 'Kiwi' Barracks on Salisbury Plain. When it came nearer to D-Day we were moved down into Brize Norton and of course everything was 'hush hush', nobody was allowed out of the camp at all, you were confined to the camp. During the time that we were in there they had models of where we were going to land. We were going to land at Ranville. Our particular thing that stands out, our assembly point was the church. We were prepared for any event and very highly trained.

The glider had skids and every glider would have held a platoon, the platoon consisted of the officer, sergeant, corporals and the men, around about thirty men and all the equipment. They were towed onto aircraft and when you

were released it was up to the pilot to take to where you were wanted. Take into account that in France they had spikes up on the fields. You trusted the man who was at the helm, and you thought 'will this stay up!' After a while you got used to it. That was your training, to get used to it. The glider was just like paper and the way they were built they could have fell into two halves. You had to get that out of your mind, if you think that way you just wouldn't want to go, but your training taught you what to do and you accepted it.

The reason for using the gliders was you were going to get in in bulk to the enemy lines. The advantage was that were going in as a battalion or a brigade to land and getting out as close as possible to the enemy.'

Marty also appreciated that there was a real and potentially devastating danger to deploying by glider.

Martin VANCE:
'The thing about casualties, when you're getting flak and getting hit; with the glider you just had no chance. It meant that instead of one or two men in a plane getting killed, you're getting twenty-three, twenty-five or maybe thirty men just falling out of the air. In that respect it was really scary.'

Belfast man Bill McCONNELL recalled the final days of training as D-Day approached, along with his own recollections of the gliders.

Bill McCONNELL:
'Well, in the weeks before D-Day we were put in a camp surrounded by a battalion, so as no-one else knew, in the New Forest. Every morning and all day long we had the village on the map, and everyone had to memorise everything that was going on all about it. We didn't have

the gliders there; we were just kept in camp and no-one was allowed to see us. That was training for about 3 or 4 weeks, to [get to] know the place where we were going to land and how we were going to land.

The gliders we went over in, there were 28 men could be taken in each glider or a Jeep with a trailer-load of ammunition and 8 men of a crew, or a Jeep and a six-pounder gun, of which there was only one for each company. All the 6 pounders were linked to one company, they were linked to 'S' company which we never seen. They were with battalion headquarters at Longueval.

A glider is made of plywood and the portholes in it are cellophane you could stick your finger through them and if you sat down hard, if you sit down hard on the seat you would've went through it. There were no safety belts, no parachute, no nothing. We had to get our head between our knees before landing and that was all we had.

[On the sixth of June] We weren't told anything. We weren't told anything at all. We were brought out onto the airfield; the gliders were lined up and each company was given a glider. First of all, I don't know if you know or not, when Major Howard went in at midnight, or in the morning, there was a glider of the 1st Battalion of the Rifles commanded by Major Drummond, they were at Herron Airdrome and unfortunately when they got into the air the towrope snapped and they couldn't go. They were all arrested by the police because they were in camouflage, and they had to get themselves certified that they belonged to us, and they managed to get themselves back to the battalion and went in with us.

The glider I was in was towed by a Dakota whereby there was two tow ropes, tow ropes from the nose of the glider to two parts of the tail of the Dakota and that's released in the air. When it's towing it just pulls you up in the air you know, like an ordinary glider. Once you're up and over the English Channel then you were released and we flew in on

our own, you can fly for miles as you know. Well, it was a beautiful, I remember as well as I am sitting here, it was a beautiful sunlit afternoon. I could see when we got over France because I could see the hospital, Caen Hospital, and the church of Ranville.'

Robert LOUGHLIN, like the other men interviewed, had served in the 70th Young Soldiers Battalion before joining the 1st Royal Ulster Rifles battalion and like his colleagues, he found himself taking part in the glider assault.

Robert LOUGHLIN:

'We couldn't go on the fourth of June because of the weather conditions but it was a 'must go' on the sixth of June. As we flew over [the channel] the sea was terrible and the lads on the boats, some of them would never make the beach. I wasn't frightened as I really didn't know what war was, what war was like. I was carrying a belt and my haversack and a water bottle. I had a .38 revolver because I was a Rangefinder and that was all, we were all dickied up and ready for action. It was quiet. Nobody talked. It was very quiet. We talked a bit when we got down, but bullets were flying through the glider and hit the angle-iron that was there to let the Jeeps and trailers in, and you heard them. If it hit the angle-iron well that was fair enough! The glider was only made of paste board, disaster. The pilot's job was a hard job. He took us off the main course and brought us in, he done a good job. If we fell into the sea you had no life belt, no nothing. All I wanted was to get down onto the ground and that was it. The glider, it looks nice enough, it looks all right but if you knew what it was made of you wouldn't get into it quite honestly. It's like plywood stuck together.

We were flying over the channel and I happened to look out, all the big ships were down below and the sea was bubbling up and I see this glider, the tail plane dragging,

and I just turned my head away. I never said a thing to the rest of the lads till this day. You see they were all hinged, and it just came down and the main part of the glider was coming down too. I turned my head away, those… with the conditions and the weather, those people would've been drowned you know. It never was mentioned. I thought it was terrible, I thought "God, get us down quick". The pilots, they kept away from the fire and came in from Breville, there was a bit of fire but not much.'

Sam LOWRY provides us with a further description including the precautions adopted to ensure that the men could actually exit the glider on landing, a landing which could only really be described as a crash landing.

Samuel LOWRY:
'The Horsa Glider, which was the one used by the infantry held about 27 to 29 men. That was three sections and a headquarters and the two glider pilots. There was very little instrumentation that I could see in the cockpit. There was the one exit and if you were hit by flak… well actually you were carrying phosphorus grenades yourself, they could go off, anything could happen at all. Surprisingly enough many of the gliders landed just dead on. We sat facing each other and usually the platoon commander sat next to the pilot and usually the platoon sergeant with the fire axe in his hand and the handcart containing the spare ammunition. It was a small handcart, two wheels, and when the ramp of the glider came down it dropped down. There was a big fire hatchet behind the pilot and we used to get that for the landing because the skid on the glider sometimes came in on top of you along with the handcart, so we were all prepared. Once we grounded, if the pilot got in between the poles – the German fields were studded with telegraph poles to stop gliders, but our glider pilot used the poles to get

the nose of the glider in between and the two poles used to brake. The object then was to see if we could spot where we were going. The landing – out quick – defensive positions. The landing itself for me on D-Day was very quiet. We were to go over the River Orne to the right flank of the British Army and the Regiment was the right-hand side of that flank. When we arrived in, we had two objectives in mind. The last one was Longueval and the first one was Ranville.

Actually sometimes I think, it's like getting a needle stuck in your arm. Sometimes you may go into a bit of a daze… I'm not saying I went into a daze but what I was rehearsing in my mind was the positions we were to take up and what I was going to do if we came through with, say, twenty-seven men. My mind was running through all these things but to say I felt an exhilaration where the adrenalin was flowing, well no it wasn't. It was sort of like being in a stupor. Once we hit land that was a different matter entirely. Fear, yes, I felt fear. The men were quiet, the odd one made a wee sickly joke but to go right down 27 men and for me to say one fellow was anticipating and one was shaking, I couldn't say that, and what was going through my officer's mind? He was probably thinking what am I going to do when we get ashore here? How are they going to perform? Maybe a myriad of thoughts and maybe something different going through your head completely, somebody at home? It was hard to say. To be conscious of fear, to acknowledge that fear, I feel is a great thing.'

Bill McCONNELL:

'I could see when we got over France because I could see the hospital, Caen Hospital and we seen the church of Ranville, you couldn't see the sea for all the ships. We didn't think anything actually, only in our own minds what was ahead for us. Our orders that morning were to hold, no matter what casualties, to hold that place [Ranville]. What I was thinking was to get down safe because we had already done

so many of these things before, but we done it with wheels we had never done this before with the chute [landing skid]. We had our head down between our legs, to take away the impact. Well, we heard machine gun fire outside Caen, near the hospital. The chateau, a big chateau that we took afterwards when we sent a patrol out and we managed to take that, to cut down the firepower on us. But ours was a simple and easy landing. Well the impact's like a very tough impact when it just hits the ground, it's supposed to do a... you see when the glider takes to the air it has two wheels and the wheels are dropped. Underneath the glider is a skid and the glider is supposed to land on that skid, and it is supposed to land flat. But with all the fields and the hedgerows we couldn't, so the one we were in, the skid hit the hedgerow and we just turned up. Then we were all thrown from the back of the glider up to the front of the glider on top of the pilots and the Jeep. The Jeep, I was the driver, the Jeep and trailer was hanging over the top of us. They were shackled in by chains, but you could have lifted the floorboards, if we had've stayed there for much longer the chains could've snapped and the whole thing fell on top of us.

Well, we managed to cut the Jeep and that out. There were gliders landing all over the place and we had to first re-group. I managed to get my Jeep and the trailer out. In the trailer we used to carry the men's, we had airborne handcarts to carry the men's haversacks and their blankets. In the Jeep we had mostly extra ammunition and mortars, 2-inch mortars and 3-inch mortars. Well, there was a big wood there and we all made for the wood. That's where we started getting ourselves together.'

Robert LOUGHLIN's landing exposed him straight away to the horror of war. He was a witness and also a party to an incident that played on his conscience and haunted him for the rest of his days.

Robert LOUGHLIN:
'When I landed, along with the rest of the boys, there was a young fellow who had just joined. He got out of the glider and I said, 'Where's your rifle?' And he said, 'In the glider.' I had to tell him that if the officer sees you, you'll be in trouble. He went in [to the glider] and what happened was there must have been a mortar bomb or a shell and it hit just on top of the glider, and you heard the ammunition on the trailer bursting, that was it, that was him finished. I didn't even know his name. As far as I was concerned, I was terrible sorry at sending him in. It stands by me to this very day. He was the first. This was a young fellow, I'm sure if he was 18 that was it. Now that stayed in my mind, I had to try and forget about it. I was only trying to keep him right by getting his gun. Whether it was a mortar or a shell it was just the one, and he went in and that was it, I'll never forget that. He was a wee lad; I took an awful pity of him after. Personally, I think war is stupid.'

Just minutes after landing on French soil Robert had been a witness to the first man of the 1st (Airborne) Battalion of The Royal Ulster Rifles to be killed in action. Rifleman John WOODBURN, as Robert recalled, was indeed a young fellow at just 19 years of age.[4] He came from Manchester in Lancashire. With the intensity of the fire and the exploding ammunition that had been carried on the trailer still on board, John Woodburn's body could not be recovered from the burning wreckage of the Horsa glider. He is to this day recorded as being 'missing in action' on the 6th June 1944. He is remembered on the Bayeau Memorial to The Missing which bears the names of some 1800 other men who died in Normandy and who have no known grave. His name is carved close to that of Jim WHITEHORN, who was killed a few hours earlier on board the SS *Sambut*. Riflemen Whitehorn and Woodburn were,

4 Commonwealth War Graves Commission www.cwgc.org/find-records/find-war-dead/casualty-details/2628796/john-woodburn/ accessed 23 Nov 2023.

remarkably, the first and only fatalities suffered across both Royal Ulster Rifles battalions on D-Day, yet owing to the circumstances of their deaths they became the first two men to be recorded as 'missing in action'.

3

The Seaborne Landings

West of The River Orne
Sword Beach

Stanley BURROWS, Hamilton LAWRENCE and Richard KEEGAN, like so many of the young men in the Royal Ulster Rifles, had enlisted through the 70th Young Soldiers' Battalion before transferring into the regular battalions. In June 1944 all three men were attached to the 2nd Battalion. As such they were destined to take part in the beach landings on the Normandy coast close to the town of Ouistreham at a location which, from the 6th June 1944 until this day, is now known universally by its Operation Overlord code name, Sword Beach, regardless of any French name it may have had.

The three men eventually trained together; initially though Stanley Burrows, from the Castlereagh area of Belfast, had volunteered for and was accepted into the 1st (Airborne) Battalion of the Royal Ulster Rifles. He trained with the 1st Battalion for a year until an intervention meant he joined the others in the 2nd Battalion.

Stanley BURROWS:
'We were all up at Plymouth at this time and they asked for volunteers for Burma and a whole crowd jumped forward. Then they asked for volunteers for the Commandos, and I was one of the ones who jumped forward then all the

ones who were going to go to Burma all jumped forward as well and changed their minds! Of course, we were too late and I didn't get in on time. The next thing they asked was volunteers for the first battalion, the Airborne and I leapt forward then too, and I was accepted for the first battalion of the gliders. I served with them for a year, and I had a perforated ear drum which I had managed up to this to hide. But then I went on a parachute course up to Ringway and it was just after I'd done six or seven weeks of para training when they discovered this perforation in my ear. I hadn't known that it was my mother [who] had written behind my back and had told them, she didn't want her wee son getting into action and getting killed. So, I was drafted out of them, never to be up in the air again, because the gliders, they also sent me away, and I ended up in the 2nd Battalion. But there was three of us went through all this together, we were known as 'The BBC', because of our surnames, BURROWS, BECK and CRANGLES. We served quite a lot, from the Young Soldiers, right through the Airborne and now into the 2nd Battalion, The Royal Ulster Rifles. We were never apart, thick and thin.'

The men of the 2nd Battalion moved through various military training camps as their training intensified during 1943 and into 1944. Although the men were not told how or where they would eventually be deployed it became obvious that their eventual role would involve some kind of beach assault as their training concentrated on the detailed aspects of an amphibious deployment.

Hamilton LAWRENCE:

'We were down in England, down on the South coast. The story was that were going to Sicily, a landing in Sicily. The Canadians were here for two or three years, and they were going nowhere. They changed the plans and sent them

and then they decided that the 3rd Division had a more difficult task to do but they never said what and that started the training. We were sent up to Scotland, we went to a place called Hawick, that was our camp, we lived in an old mill. We had a good time there. During the winter we went away up to, they say Inverary in the books but that was the Headquarters, we were away up in a place called Acharacle away up in the north of Scotland near Lough Long. They had a big boat there in the lough and they had all the equipment, all the ropes for climbing up and down. You went away onto the islands and did your training there. You lay for days after coming out of the water, because you had to go into the water. Then you did all of your exercises and training there, two or three days in trenches. It was rough then, really rough in the winter.

It was really bad because you came straight out of the water, and you had to not change for two or three days. You got food and all, but you were route marching all over the hills, through the swamps and all. You had no cover – nothing, just lying there, trenches and all. We stayed there for a long time and did all our training. It was really rough, commando training but they didn't call it commando training. That's where they did train the Commandos and they were up there, but they called it Landing Infantry Training. It was rough then, so it was, but when we got back to Hawick, we enjoyed ourselves there. We were infantry so we had to do this training because the support we had was just Bren gun carriers, no tanks or anything, just a mortar platoon, and the idea was to toughen us all up to let us know what it was about, even if we did get stranded anywhere. We had to really get on the landing, off the boat. We had to go straight into the water, it was tough training.'

Richard KEEGAN:
'We moved up to Hawick in Scotland and we were stationed in a big mill. We moved from there up to Inverary and we

did an awful lot of training on assault courses, climbed mountains and done landings. The landings that we did then, we would have went out on the boat, climbed down the netting and into the small landing craft, the one with the drop front. Any landings that we made in Scotland the beaches were firm. We also done training in a place called Acharacle in Scotland. We used to work between Inverary and Hawick and done these landings.

Then the talk was that we were to do a landing in North Africa, well it was only rumoured throughout the battalion like, never anything official. Anyway, we got embarkation leave and moved from Hawick down to Droxford. We used to go into the big tent and the whole beachhead was laid out in front of you there, all the buildings, the sand, and where the boats would have pulled in. It was always, according to Mr. Greene [Lt. Greene] "We're going on a big scheme". We would have went in there three or four days in a week and that picture funnily still sits in front of my mind and yet, whenever I've gone back [to Normandy] the picture is different.'

Stanley BURROWS:

'We moved up into the hills in Scotland and away down by Inverness direction. It was in the mid-winter and it was really tough going kind of weather. We had to cross over rivers, climb up the side of 'The Ben' in Scotland and we exercised right up those hills. It was really hard tough training. The training was harder even than what it was going in on D-Day. We were out there for about ten days and all of a sudden it rained, very very heavily. General Montgomery was there and he said, 'This is what I want, I want to see what you're like when you're in real trouble'. The muck was clinging, and we had to push and shove at vehicles to get them out of it. We also had to dig in at night and sleep in those conditions while we were there. The rations weren't like the soldier's [sic] today, they were

big square hard biscuits. We called them dog biscuits and you had to soak them before you could have digested them. That was the kind of tough training that we had, and the men were very hardy. We were ready to go, and we were told that we were training for the Sicily landings but at the last minute it was cancelled, General Montgomery said 'I want this Division to go to the D-Day landings.' We didn't know anything about it then, dates or anything like that.

I know it was tough going but I was young and hardy in those days and I actually enjoyed it, I enjoyed soldiering. I went on to serve for some 59 years. It was in my blood, and I really enjoyed it, tough and all as it was.

We went through rivers sometimes and the rivers were actually frozen at that time of the year, in the winter, and when you went through you had to get in and break the ice. They were only about eight feet to go across them, as if you were in the real thing, and we enjoyed that. We put in attacks at different places, we also had landing craft there, they were smaller ones than what we went in on on D-Day, but we made attacks on those beaches against false enemy. There were big tins and different things set on the mountain and we had to fire at these.

When you were going into these mock attacks you had to crawl on your belly and the sergeant majors in their usual sergeant major voice would have been yelling at you for all they were worth 'Keep your backside down!' Because they were firing live ammunition over the top of your heads. Montgomery's theory was to get us used to all the noise and banging, the only thing they stopped short at was hand grenades. They threw 'thunder-flashes' instead. He said, 'Get all the noise you can, because that's what breaks men down in battle.' It's the noise sometimes more than anything. They get fatigued and they can't stick the constant shelling and the constant mortaring, and they break down and have exhaustion. Many people had opinions of Montgomery as a showman but to the troops who knew him personally

and well, he was our hero. He inspired us, he gave us that courage to go forward and we looked up to him in a real way. We saw what he already had done in Italy and that meant an awful lot to us, to get encouragement from a man who had already led people to victory.

It was very tough in the winter; these seas were very rough and tough going and when they took us in to these landings we were soaking wet to the skin. Many a time you were lying shivering with cold in the nighttime as you lay. You had to dig in and Montgomery said, 'Keep your shovel and your pick-axe handy'. You would have been moaning and groaning about having to dig a trench every time you moved. If you only attacked, even on an exercise, fifty or twenty yards that would have been a 'dig in' again, right away. He [Montgomery] proved to be right because even if you were only down a foot it gave you shelter when the mortars and shelling came over. That was a very valuable lesson we learned from him there, to dig in. It did make us very hardy I'll say that we were fit, we were young soldiers, and we couldn't wait to get into action.

We didn't know that we were for the D-Day landings, at that time when we were doing all the mountain exercises and all, we thought it was for Sicily. We actually helped to load the boats for the men at Dieppe, but we were told that we were being kept for Sicily. We didn't know about D-Day until we had done Exercise Fabius[1], that was one of the toughest exercises we did before we went into action. We went away up to this place called Littlehampton where we went out on these ships. There was a big heavy escort of R.A.F. and Naval transport because the Americans had been hit [in training] at 'The Sands' I think they called them, and they lost an awful lot of life, so they weren't

1 Exercise Fabius was a practice exercise for the D-Day landings conducted in May 1944 a few weeks after a similar exercise named Exercise Tiger was conducted off the Devonshire coast at Slapton Sands in England. During Exercise Tiger hundreds of US soldiers were killed when the exercise was compromised and attacked by German motor launches.

taking that chance again. So, we went in there and we made this landing, and it was a very very rough day, the waves were coming over the sides of the boats. We landed at Littlehampton and you'd have thought you got a preview of the D-Day landings and what it would be like. We didn't know then, but it was almost like the real thing. As a matter of fact, some of the people thought that it was a commando raid coming in from the German side. It was a very tough exercise.'

During the final stages of their training in late May 1944 the men of the 2nd Battalion expressed feelings similar to those experienced and recounted by their airborne colleagues. They were kept in the dark as to an exact deployment day but nevertheless a quiet tension built within them as they each realised what was about to take place. Ultimately their fate was the same, both airborne and seaborne troops were to land on enemy occupied territory and that landing, no matter how they rationalised it within themselves, would be opposed. They were going into battle. As Jimmy Bowden explained in basic terms, 'In the end It didn't matter [about how we were trained] whether it was plane or glider or boat, that was just a way of getting you there.'

Stanley BURROWS:
'We were moved up to a place called Droxford, outside Portsmouth. The whole area was [covered with] trees and there was a powerful army of trucks and all descriptions of weapons and artillery, and everything was hidden under those trees. While we were in there the place was sealed up and nobody was allowed in or out, even the men who came to entertain us, to do the singing and the concerts and the NAAFI staff, everybody was closed in until after the D-Day landings took place. While we were in there we had big scale sand models with the different landing craft on them and the different model soldiers placed out. This was to give you

a preview of what the landings would be like. The officers in charge of doing this had put it over so well that actually when we landed on the D-Day beaches we thought we had been there before. Place names were changed, names like Poland, Mexico and Belfast and all were code names for the places where we were going to land, like Caen became maybe Poland and another place would be Belfast, these were all codes, and we knew them all off by heart. There were sealed orders that only a very few knew, the top men like Colonel Harris, they knew the actual places where we were going to be, but they weren't opened until we were halfway out to sea and then it was revealed. Everything that they did in that camp was so real that as I say, when we went on D-Day we thought we had been there before.'

D-Day Minus Two

Extract from the War Diary of the 2nd Battalion, Royal Ulster Rifles dated 4th June 1944 states, 'LCI (Landing Craft Infantry) parties proceeded from Waterlooville for loading at Southsea but returned to Camp A7 at Waterlooville, loading having been postponed for 24hrs owing to bad weather.'[2] In a similar way to their Great War predecessors awaiting the word to advance on the 1st July 1916 at Thiepval the Riflemen had been brought to a point of readiness only to be stood down to wait for the weather. On this occasion though, as reflected in the War Diary entry signed off by Colonel Ian Harris, the stresses of being brought to that point of readiness were confined to the senior officers. The rank and file, even at that late hour, were unaware that they had almost been sent to France.

Hamilton LAWRENCE:

'At about ten o'clock, nighttime on the 4th we had all got down, we were took down in trucks and we got on the landing craft. We were all set then, I'd got my bicycle and

2 The National Archives, WO 171/1384, War Diary, 2nd Royal Ulster Rifles.

got sitting down and we went away out to sea, I forget about times, I didn't look at the time. Then all of a sudden there was all the water and waves, a storm so they never said nothing, they just turned us back. It was just more or less like an exercise, they turned us back and took us back to the camp and said 'Stay there but no lying down, just keep all your gear, leave it beside you ready to put on again. Then the next morning, at daylight we had to put it back on and we went out again but this time we were lucky enough to stay on. What stopped us was that it wasn't suitable for the beaches because it was too rough, and we were going to get taken off course. They needed the moon, and it was cloudy, they had to get everything clear.

When we were out at sea we were just sitting there rolling and rolling, it was cold sitting on the sea there and it was rough, you could feel the waves coming over the top. People were sick but they had bags to be sick in so they were just sick in the bag then chucked it over into the sea. There was quite a lot of people sick. If we had have went that day, half of them wouldn't have been able to get off the boat it was that rough. We didn't know anything, we were just turned round, we didn't know it was cancelled because we didn't know what was going on. We thought that it was maybe a routine rehearsal. We just sat then in the transit camp, the lorries were all there, the transport was all there and each platoon was sitting waiting to board. You weren't allowed to sleep or anything, just to sit there waiting on the order to move off. I just remember sitting there having a smoke, we never bothered much, nobody had anything to say, we just kept silent unless somebody came out with a joke.'

D-Day Minus One

Richard KEEGAN:
'We got on board the boats, but the weather was that bad that we all had to get off the boats and back again to

Droxford. Then on the 5th June we got back on the boats and everything was laid on. We were given writing paper and envelopes to write letters home and we weren't allowed to put in anything that we were going to do, it was all personal stuff between you and your family. The letters were taken off us because they all had to be censored. On the boats then we had bunks, and we were able to take our equipment off and lie down. Some of us slept, I slept well that night. The crossing was simple enough, the bunks were underneath, and you could take your kit off and the bikes, they were left on top. We had a meal on board but most of us lay down and wrote the letters home. The next morning, we got the shout to get up and get on us, so the boots were put on and the equipment was put on. I think I had a cup of tea before we moved off.'

Stanley BURROWS:
'When we got onto the ships, I think it was a whole company at once got onto the landing craft, one of the very big ones. We got onto the landing craft, and we went down below, we were like sardines! The way we were packed into them there were bunks three high and there were bunks just to your left and to your right, if you'd fell out of your bunk you would have fallen into another fella's. Going over, at the start it was a wee bit smooth, but it got rougher as we went out, the weather was tough. On the boat the food was good. They gave us one good last meal, in case that was the last one we might get for some days. They gave us good food, fresh vegetables, and things like that. On the trip over there was a certain amount of tension, not fear but tension. We were young lads; we were dying to get into action and we couldn't wait to land. A point came when we were told we could write a letter home, but it wouldn't be posted until after the D-Day landings. Writing these letters was a bit sad. It was sad for me because I can remember to this day writing to my mother and telling her how much I loved her, telling the

family and all…things that I should have told them when I was living amongst them. You were a wild young lad and you wanted to leave the books clear and leave with a good conscience.

These things were sad, writing on the boat. In the first World War my grandmother had lost her son, missing on the Somme and I couldn't help thinking would I be one and how would my mother take it and how would she feel. I had said in the letter that if anything happened to me, I had hoped that she would go on in life, the way she always did, with a nice, good smile on her face and remember that I was only one of thousands and just be proud that her son had died for his country. It wasn't easy to write, I felt very emotional, but once I got the letter written and sealed, I felt a bit happier. At least I had said something to her. Knowing that my father had been in the first World War, he had won the Distinguished Conduct Medal, I was very, very proud of him, and I knew that he would have had a good idea of what I was going through. When I told him I had joined the Royal Ulster Rifles he said, 'You'll be in all the muck and dirt of the day.' Other than that, everyone was in very high spirit and couldn't wait to get into that landing.'

D-Day, Sword Beach, 10.00hrs

Richard KEEGAN:
'We got up on top, and formed into sections there for both ramps. I said to Corporal Kohler, "What time is it Johnny?" He took out the army issue [watch] and said, "Ten o'clock". Yet, I have seen all of these different times in different books, eleven o'clock and all the rest, now whether they were talking about French time, that would make the difference as they were always an hour ahead of us in summertime. I wasn't panicking, I wasn't excited, nothing in that line at all, in fact I didn't see anybody panicking, everybody seemed to be quite cool, as the officer had said [Lt. Greene], "You're going

on a big scheme." I never saw anything out of the ordinary as regards that. Everybody turned round when they lined up on top of the boat and gathered their bike, put their rifle or Bren gun or whatever they were carrying, where it wasn't going to get wet. There were a lot of ships stranded on the beach which meant that other boats that were coming in to make the landings at the same time as us couldn't get in. They had to wait until our boat pulled out and then pull in because there were a whole lot of them beached. They were the smaller ones too; they must have been the ones that did the landing. If you got in you got in, if you didn't... some of the boats loaded further out than us, they were wading through the water chest deep, same as us.

As we came in to make our landing the battleships that were out there were firing over our heads, where the shells were landing, I do not know but there was a gun point at Ouistreham and they were firing at it because it was firing onto the beach. But then there must have been other weapons somewhere back further doing the same thing. I grabbed my bike, my bike was different from all of the rest, I had one of these... the others had folding bikes, mine wasn't a folding bike. I just got my rifle, wrapped the sling around the handlebar, put the butt onto the seat, hoisted it onto my shoulder and held onto the rifle so that it wouldn't come off and into the water. That left the other hand free. I just walked down the ramp, into the water. I walked onto the beach and went to run but I couldn't run because I was sliding all over the place, it was like walking in snow. Eventually I made it up the ramp and into the wee side street. On the landing the Engineers had cleared gaps through the metalwork that the Germans had put up to protect them, they had mines tied up to them, so you were beat no matter what way you went, only them fellas [engineers] had opened the gap for you. Also, behind that they had the barbed wire so they opened that gap for you to walk through and get off the beach as quick as you could. We moved from there up to

where they called 'The Orchard' and we had a roll call there and everything was in order.'

Hamilton LAWRENCE:

'Everything was quiet and then when the dawn broke, we looked up, we wondered where the noise was coming from, we knew it was planes but we didn't know where they were coming from, whether it was the enemy planes our ours. I looked up and I seen all of them, everybody was happy, smiling you know. It perked everybody up, they knew what was happening then, amazement, the landing craft all around and the ships back at sea. It was amazing, it transformed everybody and made everybody happy then. We were prepared and we were looking forward to getting off the boat more than anything else. A lot of the men were sick as we were never used to the sea, a lot of them were seasick but they had plenty of time to be seasick and get settled, it calmed down as we got nearer to the beaches. Everybody was seasick you might as well say because a lot of them had to stand, there was no room, and we were sitting on the packs with all of your equipment with you. They got relaxed when they saw what was happening, the support that they were going to have.

When we got near, when we got to maybe about half a mile out from the beach, we could see what was happening and we could see the rest of the Brigade and their landing craft in front of us. It was just a whole crowd in front like a triangle going in and they went in first. We stopped out a bit until they all, the other brigades went in first. We couldn't all go in together. Then our brigade went in last, the second one, we went in at about ten or eleven o'clock in the morning. We got shell fire and sniper fire but not much. Just before we got onto the beach, we were crushed trying to get off with all of our equipment and all on. Our whole aim was to get off that landing craft as quickly as possible because the sniper fire and the shells were coming

in. We knew we weren't going to be safe sitting there and everybody was crushing to get off. It was first off quick, no matter what way they got off. It was amazing, it was a right mad rush to get off it.

Then, when we were actually coming in the pilot said that he had hit the wrong bit [of the beach]. He hadn't hit the wrong bit, but he didn't expect the tide to be where it was. The other battalion platoons were on the right and left of us. As soon as the ramp went down, we knew right away that nobody was going to get into that water because the first ones that went in went in right up to their heads and they wouldn't let anybody get off. One of the sergeants, Sergeant McCutcheon and another big, tall chap took lines and they managed to get them tied on to the barriers that the Germans had, they managed to get them tied round them. The engineers were there as well and with Sergeant McCutcheon they took the lines straight out and they got one from each craft in our battalion and managed to take them off that way, just holding onto the line, but you were up to your neck. It was actually five feet deep in places and more than four feet right through to the beach. You had all your equipment and then you had a bicycle on one arm and some people had a Bren guns and mortars all on their shoulders and picks and shovels. It was really laughable, but we managed to get off though we were soaking wet, and we stayed that way the whole time, never got dried out and no change of clothes in that time. When we got onto the beach then the Engineers had cleared a path for us. We were expecting mines and that on the beach and we had to go through all of the defences, barbed wire and concrete defences. We had to go in single file on a path, like a country path on a field. When we got on the beaches the Engineers were sitting there waiting to get the landing craft back home again as quickly as possible and they were waving 'cheerio' to us.

Stanley BURROWS:

'On the way over it began to get very rough and the ship was bobbing up and down because they were flat bottomed, and they were bobbing up and down all kinds and the weather got real rough. We had over 56lb of gear on our backs. We had a bicycle, every single man from the Commanding Officer down had a bicycle and I had a machine gun, a Bren gun and other men had the mortars, so they were that bit heavier to try to get off the boat. When we were getting in the boat was going up and down and rocking about a lot more but when we looked out there all around us was ships like H.M.S. *Belfast* and the *Warspite*, there was just a big armada of ships. The whole sea was a sort of black with ships and the air was just covered with aircraft of every description, bombers, gliders, the airborne going over, the parachutists going over, and it was a tremendous feeling that you had such support when you saw that overhead and you had that around you. You felt almost that nothing could touch you but yet you knew that one shell from that beach could put you up in the air for life. It was a tremendous feeling to look up and see all this around you.

I remember well the first shelling, there were a few shells came in from the Germans and they delayed our convoy a bit, but the convoy got back set again and the next thing we heard was this terrific blast of fire and it was from the H.M.S. *Belfast*. Our Company Commander then, Major Tighe-Wood said, "By God, that's the Belfast!" He had recognised it, most of the rest of us didn't as we had never seen it before, but he did. So, we went in with this powerful escort around us, behind us, surrounding us and leading us in. As we got nearer the beach and we saw the beaches coming into view, it was so clear from the models and the training we had done at Droxford that we thought we had been there before. It was so life-like. When we got in close to the beach the ship that I was on, it was number 697, had been hit by a shell just before we went in. Some of the men

that were on it didn't even know, it was just like a 'thud'. It passed straight through the hull and never exploded, thank God or I wouldn't be here today to tell you this story.

She set down in about 8 feet of water. Now 8 feet of water is enough to drown any man when you've got 56 lb of gear and a Bren gun and a bicycle and all that. You'll go down to Davy Jones' locker, and you wouldn't rise too easy! I looked at that and I knew that there was a man once walked on the sea and I wasn't him and I knew that if I tried to walk on that sea, down I would go. So, I just lifted the bicycle and threw it over the side, that was a wee bit lighter. That left me with the Bren gun and my gear. There was a Sergeant-Major Welsh and Rifleman Ryan who had won a Military Medal in Dunkirk, they had managed to get ashore and got a rope tied onto our boat and I put the rope underneath my arm and held the Bren gun – I used to call it 'Betsy' not after any girl in particular, it was just a habit I had, I used to tap it and say "Betsy, don't let me down now" meaning don't be having a stoppage, keep firing. I had it over my shoulder and I said "Betsy, you're going to get baptised". When we were pulling ourselves ashore the water was just splashing right over your head, and I was actually up to my neck holding onto the rope. If I'd have let go, I'd have gone down deep into the water. I managed to get my feet to the ground and as we made our way in there was a large volley of shells and mortar fire all falling on the beach.'

Stanley Burrows, in his account of the landing recalls that there were no casualties or men drowned at sea. He does however intimate that there were rumours of Royal Ulster Riflemen being drowned during the D-Day landings which he dismissed. What he heard from others in subsequent years may have originated from the accounts of the fate of rifleman Edwin WHITEHORN of the 2nd Royal Ulster Rifles who we now know was killed at sea. Stanley Burrows, like many others, was unaware of what happened

earlier that morning on board the SS *Sambut*. He quite correctly states that no men from the battalion were lost during the actual beach assault.

Stanley BURROWS:

'I must say at this point that we didn't have anyone drown at sea. Some men have made the statement that there were Rifles drowned at sea. There were no Ulster Rifles drowned or lost their lives in the water. We all managed to get ashore, but we had casualties. We had men hit with mortar fire and some with sniper fire. We had very very good sniper teams. We had one man who was a Bisley shot, and he was good at taking out the snipers.'

The Bicycles: Aside from the Germans, one common enemy, as we have heard now from both airborne and seaborne troops on D-Day was the bicycle. Stanley explained their intended use and ultimate fate.

Stanley BURROWS:

'The reason for each one of us having a bicycle was that they believed that the Germans would retreat very fast when we landed, and they thought that we would need the bicycles to keep up with them. They thought that we would take Caen in one day, it turned out to be months. They had these bicycles to get after the Germans very fast, but the Germans were a good fighting soldier, although we didn't like some of them, they were good fighting soldiers and they had no intention of retreating as fast as that. I made the decision on the boat that I couldn't get off with all that weight and I needed at least one hand free to hold the rope and that hand was holding the bicycle; so, the bicycle went over the side. These bicycles were all folding bicycles. They folded in two with a nut in the middle to keep them that way. Some of the men from the other boats in not as deep water and

some of ours even managed to get ashore with their bicycles and they actually took them as far as Cambes. Others were thrown on the roadside and tanks went over them, what was left the French people pinched because they hadn't much means of transport. The Germans weren't going to retreat that fast and I didn't need it. It didn't prove to be such a vital bit of equipment after all.'

On landing the Riflemen made their way off the eastern edge of Sword Beach at a point designated as 'Exit 11'. From there they made their way inland through Lion-sur-Mer and then to a location where they had named 'The Orchard' which was in nearby Hermanville-sur-Mer. Here they regrouped and met up with their reconnaissance section, commanded by Captain Ryan, who had landed one hour ahead of the main body of the battalion with elements of the Headquarters Company. While still under sporadic mortar and sniper fire the battalion moved on before finally bivouacking around a ridge and farm buildings at Périers-sur-le-Dan. They dug in there for the night, reflected on the day and considered what lay ahead.

Although, as Stanley Burrows had pointed out, the 2nd Battalion, The Royal Ulster Rifles had not suffered any fatalities during the landing on Sword Beach they had taken casualties in the form of men wounded from shrapnel and small arms gunfire. An invaluable record of casualties was maintained by the Medical Sergeant, James Edward DRUMGOOLE. Sergeant Drumgoole was an experienced member of the Regimental Aid Post; he had enlisted in the Royal Ulster Rifles in 1932 and had served with the regiment in Sudan and later in Palestine between 1937 and 1939. Sergeant Drumgoole had taken part in the Dunkirk evacuation in 1940 and had been mentioned in despatches for his service during the evacuation operation. Jim Drumgoole had drawn from his experiences and was aware, perhaps more than most, of the importance attached to the accurate recording of the details of the

men treated for wounds and illness along with the grim task of recording the battalion fatalities. On the 6th June 1944 he opened a fresh, blank Public Service Stationery Office book and began recording the details of the battalion casualties. He continued this task right until the battalion crossed the Rhine in March 1945. The book was eventually lodged with the Royal Ulster Rifles Museum in Belfast where it became known simply as 'The Drumgoole Roll'. To a researcher it has provided a uniquely detailed document of the result of the actions of the battalion, often cutting through the 'fog of war' and laying out the grim reality of the extent and nature of battle casualties. On the 6th June 1944 Sergeant Drumgoole recorded ten casualties, three on Sword Beach and the remaining seven as a result of sniper and mortar fire at The Orchard at Hermanville.

As D-Day came to an end both battalions of The Royal Ulster Rifles had successfully gained a foothold in occupied France. Their total fatalities amounted to two men.

4

D-Day Plus One:
East of the Orne

Ranville

By 00.00hrs on the 7th June 1944 Battalion Headquarters for the 1st (Airborne) Battalion of the Royal Ulster Rifles had been established just south-west of the village of Ranville on the eastern bank of the Orne Canal. The men of the battalion had regrouped on landing at the church located just south of the landing zone, the spire of which had been used as a navigational aid for the incoming glider pilots. On regrouping the men dug in to defensive positions nearby, organised in their various companies, and awaited further orders. Opposition had been slight following the initial landings and had diminished to sniper fire during the early hours. By all accounts the German 7th Army, who were responsible for the defence of Normandy, had been taken by surprise. An analysis of translations of their telephone signals for the period builds a picture of a fragmented initial response to what was a full-scale Allied invasion. The German 716th Infantry Division had reacted to the first reports of airborne landings on the 6th June but an assessment had been made that these were isolated raids. This assessment was compounded by the use of dummy parachute troops which were deployed at Carpiquet Airfield. The two formations best placed to reinforce the 716th Division were the 21st Panzer Division, essentially Rommel's old

Afrika Corps, along with the 12th SS Hitlerjugend or Hitler Youth Panzer Division. The 21st Panzer Division were initially ordered to the area east of the River Orne which would have placed them in direct opposition to the lightly armed Airborne troops which included the 1st RUR.

At 16.20hrs on the 6th June, the German Chief of General Staff reported to the Chief of the 7th Army Group that the 21st Panzer Division had reinforced the 716th Infantry Division with advance units probing north of Caen.[1] The 21st Panzer Division were diverted from attacking east of the Orne to west of the river on the orders of General Jodl who directed that all available forces were to be directed to the assessed point of penetration, namely in the direction of Bayeux. By 22.40hrs on the 6th June the Commander in Chief of the 7th Army made a situation report to Field-Marshal Rommel. In it he informed Rommel that the attack by the 21st Panzer Division was halted by increased allied airborne landings and that the location of the 12th SS at that time was unknown. It was therefore decided that preparations were to be made for a counterattack on the 7th June north of Caen with the 21st Panzer Division supported by troops from the Panzer Training Corps on the German right flank and the 12th SS Hitlerjugend on the left flank. It was reported at this time that elements of the 716th Infantry Division were holding out in various strong points east and west of the Orne but as recorded in the signals, *'There is no more communication between divisional, regimental and battalion headquarters so that nothing is known of events, or which strong points are still intact. Counterattack on June 7 must at all costs reach the coast as the defenders of strong points are expecting this of us.'* For the men of the 1st and 2nd Royal Ulster Rifles their fate had been sealed as they each, ultimately, were destined to face different

---

1   RAF Historical Branch, Translations from Captured German Documents 'Air Operations on the Western Front 1942-1945 https://www.raf.mod.uk/our-organisation/units/air-historical-branch/ahb-german-translations/ accessed 24 Mar 2023.

elements of the same foe, each with their respective consequences. At Ranville the strategic decisions debated by the German High Command, for the short term at any rate, meant little to the Riflemen as they settled into their first night in occupied France.

Sam LOWRY:

'It seemed to be very quiet, when I say quiet, as a soldier going in you expect to hear gunfire, you'd have heard a bit of shelling going down, but it wasn't in the immediate vicinity. It didn't pin you down. To me actually, the first night, I had a bit of sleep. We sort of got ready to take our attacks the next day. D-Day itself to me was rough but it sort of way was partly a dream to me. Don't get me wrong, I was conscious of the shooting and all around me, but it just passed over. Sometimes you do things and later on when you look back on it, it seems as though it was a dream. At that particular point it felt very dreamy, the next day wasn't a dream, believe me, I can tell you that now. The River Orne was the dividing factor between the seaborne troops and the airborne troops, in particular the airborne troops were on the left flank of the British Army, the Rifles were on the tip of that flank and when they started to hit back, I believe it was the 21st Panzer, they were good.'

As darkness descended the initial battles fought by the battalion were often inside their own heads. The men had to come to terms with their new normal, the reality of being suddenly dropped into a hostile arena where the darkness bred fear and doubt in their abilities.

Robert LOUGHLIN:

'I didn't sleep well; I don't think I slept at all. I didn't know where I was, I knew I was beside the church. As far as I was concerned nobody gave us instructions what to do. I wasn't happy because you were always listening, you don't

know who's creeping up on you at night and we didn't know where to go or what to do. There was a whole lot of lads like me too, and officers. I was waiting for the dawn coming to tell you the truth, I felt a bit brighter at dawn and I'm sure everybody was the same as me. You were in a strange country, and you didn't know where you were in the dark; real dark it was.'

Bill McCONNELL:

'It was very eerie and everyone was to stand to first of all at dusk. We seen starshells go up and it was lighting the whole area and we dug in then. We dug in with an entrenching tool, that's just a small hand thing, it wasn't a spade and you had to dig in with that in the slit trench for safety. Some of us dug about 4 feet to get in, usually there was two of us in a trench but the one I was in was with my mate and he was on guard, and they came over and they started firing the 88mm and unfortunately, I wanted my mammy. But my mammy was dead, and I'm not afraid to admit it and I'm sure I wasn't the only one, and I know I wasn't the only one, and a captain came, and he asked me what was wrong, and he tapped me on the side of the chin and he brought me round, brought me back. If he hadn't have done that I would have been back in Antrim with about five or six others of our people. The mind just goes, the mind breaks, you're saying things and wanting things that you can't have. Well, as I say, everyone's all right until the nighttime, the Germans were at St. Honorine, not too far away from us. They started firing (the 88mm gun) and we had nothing to fire back at them with because all we had was rifles and Sten guns. I nearly broke down, I did, I started crying, I wanted my mum, and the captain came along, and he said, 'Are you all right McConnell' and I said 'No, I want my mammy.' So he just shook me and he just clipped me on the chin with the back of his hand. Not a punch, just a jest, and he hit me with the back of his hand, and it brought me round to reality,

brought me back to my senses again, let's put it that way. There used to be a thing in the first World War where people were shot for the same thing, because the mind broke. It didn't happen that way in the Second World War. The same symptoms happened but the same punishment wasn't dealt out. They started then realising that it wasn't cowardice, it was men's minds that was breaking them. I think it was just fright, because I was on my own in a foreign country. I was just realising that war was war and was different than what I thought when we were landing, completely different. Let's say, we didn't know what was in front of us and with the weapons we had as an airborne unit we were not equipped to go against a battalion of men who were highly, which we didn't realise then how highly qualified they were until the next day, until the 7th. Well, I was coming up 19, most of us came from the Young Soldiers battalion and there were none of us over the age of 18, we had all forged our birth certificates to join the army along with boys from the South of Ireland as well. I just wanted to… I wanted to be in along with the men you know. It was a major change to me, and it was to the good that I held on by just Captain Martin talking to me, I could get on and back to my senses again. I was OK after that night because I took part the next morning in an attack, a frontal attack.'

For both battalions during the initial days of the invasion one of the most effective threats came from the German Army use of snipers. One well trained and well concealed sniper was capable of holding up and to a degree dictating the movement of an infantry battalion by denying free movement across areas which had been deemed clear of the enemy. Each of the men interviewed could recall, often with clarity, their experiences in dealing with enemy snipers. At Ranville, shortly after the airborne landings two of these accounts, from men of different units describe one incident, their testimonies were not linked until years later.

Jim BOWDEN:

'I saw one bullet land about three feet from me. It was a sniper in the church tower (at Ranville). He could have hit me. A brave man because he had to have come through across the fields from Breville where his troops were and got into the church tower, he was firing all round him. So, he spotted me just around dawn or so, I heard the shooting and put my head up and I saw the bullet hitting. I was told later that somebody on the other side could see it and got into the church and got him down.'

Bill McCONNELL:

'He (the sniper) was causing a lot of trouble until he was brought down. We were moving out of Ranville to Longueval when it happened. If they hadn't have got him down, he would have destroyed us, which a sniper can, he was cutting... he was taking our people away and they were told either get him down or blow him down with the 6 pounder if they didn't get him out of the tower because the tower is very narrow at the Church at Ranville there, at the Cemetery. He was brought down... I brought him down actually, but I'd rather not talk about it. The orders were to get him down, I was a sniper as well. So, he had to be brought down. Underneath the belfry we found there was another German there and he had a foot blown off and we had a couple of (British) Paras in there who were wounded, and they are lucky we did get him down or else they would have blown that tower down. I had to do it... or else... that way. It was a thing that had to be done and I was given an order to do it... whether I felt... our own people were getting wounded, but I was given an order to do it. I was a good shot but not a crack shot. I was good enough to bring him down, well I was in a position to see where he was. I had to get into position at that time, in a position to see where he was. He was in a good position for he could have taken anyone down if they hadn't found out he was

in that tower. He was buried in the church yard there just beside it. That's where he is. I still see the grave now and again; in fact I was at it this year (2003). That was that.'

Bill McConnell began making pilgrimages to the Normandy battlefields in 1996 at a time when he was an instrumental figure in establishing permanent memorials to both the 1st and 2nd Royal Ulster Rifles Battalions located at Ranville and Cambes respectively. He returned each year and paid his respects at the German grave until the year of his death in 2020. On each visit he walked among the graves of his fellow Riflemen, his old friends, before laying a poppy wreath at the Airborne Memorial Cross in the centre of the cemetery at Ranville. On each occasion Bill then quietly made his way to the perimeter wall of the old church cemetery nearby. After walking past the still bullet-marked church and tower Bill, each year, sought out the grave of the Unknown German Warrior whom he was pitted against in a deadly duel, one on one, at dawn on the 7th June 1944. On each occasion Bill, wearing his Airborne red beret with Royal Ulster Rifles badge and serge green veteran's blazer adorned with medals earned then and since, laid a second wreath of poppies on the German grave before stepping back at attention and saluting a fallen soldier. Bill went on to serve in many campaigns with the Royal Ulster Rifles, eventually becoming the Regimental Sergeant Major of the battalion he had once lied about his age to join. He had a mutual respect for the man whose life he took, the German sniper who remained alone in the tower of Ranville Church, alone against the tide of an invasion force. In taking up his lonely position in the tower on that June morning he must have realised that his fate was sealed, his day had come, and it was only a matter of hours and minutes before he would be taken down. Bill, who had battled his own demons just a few hours before, realised that day the meaning of courage, the fragility of human life and importantly, respect. Until his final day he never forgot the man whose life he

had to take. As Bill McConnell dispatched the sniper at dawn on the 7th June 1944 his day had just begun.

Contact had been established between the commander of the 1st Royal Ulster Rifles and the local French Resistance fighters, formally known as the Forces Françaises de L'Intérieur or F.F.I. Intelligence on German troop movements and numbers was passed to the commanders on the ground although outside of any formal arrangement with F.F.I. operatives the general French public were apprehensive and cautious of actively engaging with the British soldiers until it became clear that they were there to stay. German reprisals were ruthless, anyone caught passing information to the invading forces risked arrest, torture and death. Against this backdrop, in the early hours of the 7th June 1944 Bill McConnell was approached again by Captain Martin, the 'A' Company second in command, the same officer who had swiftly brought Bill to his senses when his nerves faltered a few hours earlier. Captain Martin was obviously now certain of Bills capabilities as he singled him out along with a sergeant and three others and asked him to volunteer to accompany him on a dangerous intelligence gathering operation:

Bill McCONNELL

'The CO had asked for a recce to go in and meet the Maquis (F.F.I), the head man of the Maquis of the French to find out the strength of the enemy in Caen. It was volunteers that they asked for, you didn't have to go if you didn't want, but I wanted to go. Well, I was in the Recce Platoon and we had to go into Caen after I was brought to, that next morning when I became all right, although they were going to go without me but I wanted to go. Captain Martin was ordered to go into Caen, and he asked me did I want to go, there was five of us. He had orders from the colonel to get in and find out the strength of the German army because again they were told that the strength wasn't a big strength, that

there wasn't a lot there but when we got there, there was a garrison, and that's some soldiers I can assure you!

We got picked up by the Maquis, one of the French Resistance and he took us in his truck to the bottom of the fort. You know the fort in Caen there? We were standing at the bottom of the fort – but not for long. Captain Martin was away, we thought we had lost him, or he had been taken because he had been away for about half an hour. We had to stand there and hide there, and the Germans were walking up and down the blinking road, the main road. We were standing there, and we had to get out as quick as we could, and he took us back. That was off the scene. That was never known, this was a thing that was never put out you know, about us doing that. Over our uniform we had an old smock sort of thing, we still had our uniform on underneath. If we had've been caught that was it. But we knew the consequences, well we would have been shot. I had got rid of all the fright, I wasn't frightened then, I had just come from a boy to a man overnight.

We were just outside the Fort (in Caen) and the Germans, there were thousands of them there, our information had said there were very little (of them). It turned out the Germans were standing just above us, and we were standing, five of us, and we got then the strength of the enemy, very very strong. Apparently, we were to go in and take Caen; we would have been annihilated. I'm glad we didn't have to go in and take it that night, we would have been slaughtered.

Well, if that was now, I would think I was a bloody fool. You don't think of them things like that. I had never seen a German in reality before and we were in their midst among them, four of us. But we found out afterwards what they were. We found out to our cost on the 7th June. Well, that was the night before on the 6th of June, early 7th, but we found out to our cost on the 7th that the Germans were not playing games.'

The intelligence obtained by Captain Martin's daring reconnaissance patrol was passed to the Battalion Intelligence Officer and on to Brigade, although obtained by the 1st Battalion it was of use to the 2nd Battalion Royal Ulster Rifles who ultimately had the responsibility of taking Caen. Initially it was believed that the city could be taken within days of the invasion ultimately though the 2nd RUR did not enter the city until the 8th July and even then only after an intensive air raid was carried out. As is usual with matters of intelligence little documentation exists to indicate the detail of any report or how it was actioned by the Brigade staff. One document, held at the National Archives at Kew[2], and not released to the public until 1978 gives us a hint that there was early liaison between the 1st RUR and intelligence sources on the ground in the Ranville or Longueval area. The Military Staff College Camberley 1947 Course Notes contained detailed notes on the D-Day landings relating to the Headquarters of the 6th Airlanding Brigade of which the 1st RUR was a part. The file contains a copy of a very brief but telling intelligence return from the 1st RUR timed at 01.35hrs on the 7th June 1944. The message states: 'Have received report enemy captured one subunit of 12 Para and are wearing their uniforms.' Further references entered into the 1st battalion War Diary[3] on days subsequent to the 7th June 1944 clearly indicate that the battalion was assisted by the local doctor at Longueval, Monsieur Henri DAVOISNE and that the assistance amounted to the passing on of information relating to German patrols and strengths in the area. It could well be that Henri Davoisne was the Maquis commander who drove Captain Martin's reconnaissance patrol into Caen early on the 7th June, the 01.35hrs intelligence report certainly indicates that they had contact with a local source at the relevant time.

---

2   The National Archives, WO223/15, Staff College Camberley 1947 Course Notes, D-Day + War Diary HQ 6 A/B Div 6 – 12th June 1944.
3   Royal Ulster Rifles Museum, Bedford Street, Belfast. War Diary, 1st Bn RUR June 1944.

As for Captain Martin, mentioned by Bill McConnell, there is no doubt that he was an exceptional officer, well capable of commanding such a mission. Captain Robert Dickson MARTIN MC was appointed second in command of 'A' Company of 1st RUR before taking command of the Reconnaissance Platoon. He was initially commissioned into the regiment in June 1940 at the age of 19 years having initially served with the Artist's Rifles, a territorial officer training regimen which later evolved into the Special Air Service. He came from London and was born in Norwood in 1921. He was a consistently courageous and dynamic officer. Subsequent to his service during the D-Day landings he later took part in action with the battalion in the Ardennes in the offensive known as the 'Battle of the Bulge' and then in 'Operation Varsity' the codename for the operation that entailed the crossing of the River Rhine. He was awarded the Military Cross for a number of actions over a three-month period. The citation for the award reads:

'For continuous gallantry, conspicuous bravery in the field and complete disregard of his own personal safety. During the period 1st August to 21st October 1944 this officer commanded the Battalion Reconnaissance Platoon. During the advance from the River Orne to the River Seine the Reconnaissance Platoon was in the forefront during the whole advance and on many occasions Captain Martin, by his determination, cool leadership and conspicuous bravery, overcame many obstacles that would otherwise have held the Battalion up for a considerable time. For example, near Cabourg on 18th August 1944 the Reconnaissance Platoon led by Captain Martin came under fire from two machine guns and rifles. Owing to minefields on either side the platoon went to ground and returned fire. Captain Martin immediately laid on an attack which by its swiftness overcame the enemy. Shortly after this the Reconnaissance Platoon was held up by a determined enemy manning a Pillbox. Casualties were occurring and Captain Martin went back to

organise smoke and covering fire as well as stretcher bearers and the collection of casualties. A stretcher bearer was wounded, and Captain Martin took over the bearer's job. An hour ensued during which the wounded men were slowly dragged into some kind of cover. During this time Captain Martin was an inspiration to the entire party. The smoke lessened and the enemy mortaring grew heavier. Captain Martin then crossed the open a second time and organised further covering fire and 3' Mortar Smoke. He then returned once more and saw his casualties out and finally came out himself helping to carry a stretcher and crossing a minefield in the process. By his great courage, Captain Martin was directly responsible for inspiring his Platoon to an effort which meant the recovery of wounded, the maintenance of unity and the infliction of casualties on the enemy who started the battle from an extremely advantageous position.'

There is no doubt that Bill McConnell was inspired by this officer, being the man who steadied his nerve during that first lonely night in France. The two men served together as they fought across occupied France with Bill usually detailed as Captain Martin's Jeep driver. When studying the histories of soldiers at war we often hear of premonitions and strange turns of events where seemingly simple actions lead to unexplained consequences which cannot be rationalised. Later in the war, as Bill and Robert Martin were preparing for the airborne assault to cross the Rhine one such event occurred.

Bill McCONNELL:
'Oh, my mind is still fresh to the people I went to France with, very much so. It (D-Day) was a major victory, and I went with them to the crossing of the Rhine and they were all killed at the crossing of the Rhine. Captain Martin who was my officer, in charge of us, they were all killed in two gliders. There were fifteen gliders just shot out of the air when they did the crossing of the Rhine at Haminkeln.

My mind is just as fresh now as it was then. I can even remember, talking about going into Germany, I was with Captain Martin in the Recce Platoon, and we got onto the glider, I was the driver of the Jeep with him. He said to me 'Go back to the hangar for me I've left my night binoculars behind.' There was only eight of us, we had a Jeep and a trailer loaded with ammunition and eight of us in the glider. I went back to the hangar at the RAF base and got his binoculars and took them back to him, but he wouldn't let me back onto the glider, he said 'Go and find another glider, you're not getting on this one.' His glider was blown to pieces, everyone in it was killed. I get dreams… with a couple of drinks I'm there. I'm still there'.

The incident described by Bill took place at RAF Gosfield near Braintree in Essex on the 24th March 1945. The 1st Battalion war diary gives scant detail, 'At 00.15hrs the battalion take off on Operation Varsity/Plunder, place: Haminkeln, Germany. At 10.20hrs landing of gliders commences. Casualties for the day were 16 Officers, 243 Other Ranks.' Of that total of 259 casualties 52 were killed in action either in the air or on landing, seven others remain missing in action. Captain Robert Dickson MARTIN MC was one of the officers killed, he survived the initial crash landing and died shortly afterwards. He was buried by his men at Haminkeln before his body was moved to a final resting place at Reichswald Forest British Cemetery in November 1946. His reason for denying Bill McConnell access to the glider that morning will never be known. The fact that he did so however means that we now know of the story of the first British soldiers to enter occupied Caen on the 7th June 1944, all be it for a period of around 30 minutes, Captain Robert Dickson Martin MC, Corporal Bill McConnell, along with a sergeant and two other unknown riflemen.

It can be seen from the War Diary[4] of the 1st RUR that initial

---

4 Ibid.

intelligence was received on landing that snipers were active in the area, this was proven to be true as recounted by both Jim Bowden and Bill McConnell. Further information indicated that there were enemy troops in the nearby village of Longueval and at a location known as 'Ring Contour 30' corresponding to its position on the invasion maps supplied for the operation. The 30-metre contour line represented an area of high ground between Ranville and another nearby village, southeast of Longueval called St. Honorine. The strengths of enemy forces in those areas were not known to the Riflemen. This gap in intelligence could be attributed in some part to an unfortunate incident on the night of 5th June. It was intended that an advanced glider party containing the Battalion Second-in-Command Major J. Drummond would land then and establish a Battalion Headquarters ahead of the main landing deployment to be 'well in picture' before the battalion arrived. Unfortunately, the glider carrying the HQ party broke its tow line after take-off and was forced to land on farm land at Worthing in England. Major Drummond was able to return to the airfield with his men and take off again with the main party, any opportunity to use the time during the half day or so during D-Day to gather intelligence on enemy strengths was therefore lost.

Just before midnight on the 6th June the battalion received orders to take and hold the 'Ring Contour 30' area ahead of an attack on Longueval and St. Honorine and by 02.00hrs on the 7th June this task was completed unopposed by 'C' Company, commanded by Major F.R.A. Hynds, the enemy having previously withdrawn to St. Honorine. The best account of the attacks on the villages of Longueval and St. Honorine can be found in an appendix to the War Diary, held at the National Archives under catalogue number WO 171/5278[5], in the form of a report made by Major G. P. Rickcord of 'B' Company as follows:

---

5 The National Archives, WO171/5278 Appendix to War Diary 1st Bn The Royal Ulster Rifles.

'The plan for the capture of LONGUEVAL was briefly as follows – 'C' Coy and one pl (platoon) MMG to remain on hill 30 as fire Company. The mortars (less 'C' Coy mortars which were in position on hill 30) to get into position South of RANVILLE and support the attack. The Bn 2i/c was ordered to co-ordinate the fire support and contact the F.O.Os (Artillery forward observation officers) and F.O.B. on hill 30. The remainder of the Bn to carry out a right flanking attack on LONGUEVAL with 'B' on the right 'A' left and 'D' support 'A' Coy. Zero hour for the attack 0900 hrs.

The Bn moved to the FUP (Forming up point) without incident. In the meantime, life on hill 30 was full of incident. 'C' Coy, which had of necessity occupied hastily prepared positions in the dark, was in full view of the enemy from St. HONORINE. The range was about 1200 yards – very suitable for mortars and SP guns which opened up a heavy and relentless fire. A number of casualties were sustained. The FOO from the Fd Regt was contacted but was uncertain if he would have completed ranging by Z-15 minutes. The FOO from the Lt Regt was later contacted some distance away but stated that he could not reach hill 30 owing to the intense fire. The FOB with a call on HMS ARETHUSA was present on hill 30 but stated that (a) his wireless could not get through to the control ship and (b) that in any event he considered fire support from the Cruiser was most unlikely to be forthcoming as too many calls were already being made from other F.O.Bs. (A) The Bn mortar Officer forward in observation of hill 30 ranged his mortars and was prepared to fire on time.

Little need be said regarding the actual infantry attack on LONGUEVAL as the locality was not held by the enemy and the Bn walked straight in.

The Bn commander now decided to attack St. HONORINE forthwith leaving 'C' Coy on hill 30 and 'D' Coy (Major AJ Dyball) in occupation of LONGUEVAL – the assault to be carried out with 'A' & 'B' Coys (Maj CE Vickery and Major GP Rickcord). Orders for the attack were received on hill 30 by wireless. Zero hour was given as 11.00 hrs. The fire plan consisted of mortar concentrations

on forward edges of St. HONORINE from Z-15 minutes to Z and artillery concentration from 2-3 minutes to Z to Z+2 minutes.

The fire plan was put into effect as ordered but zero hour passed and there was no sign of the infantry advancing towards St. HONORINE. At 11.10 hrs information was received at hill 30 that zero hour had been postponed. This had become unavoidable as, owing to the instructions given by the Brigade Commander that the attack on St. HONORINE should be carried out with the least possible delay, an overoptimistic estimate had been given and sub-units had not been allowed sufficient time for preparation and the giving out of orders. As it was, even with the postponed zero hour to 12.15 hrs 'B' Coy went into the attack deficient of one platoon which was unable to reach the FUP in time. The postponement of zero hour also seriously affected the fire plan, as the mortars and MMGs had expended almost all their ammunition and there was now little time for replenishment. Determined efforts were, however, made by the mortar Officer and a small supply of ammunition was obtained. During all this time 'C' Coy was still under continuous fire from FERDINAND (88mm S.P. gun) and mortars and their casualties had not been light. A short time before zero-hour seven enemy 75mm SP guns (thought at that time to be tanks by all concerned) were seen from hill 30 to be moving from the NE towards St. HONORINE. This information was sent by wireless, with all speed, to Bn HQ but, owing to an unfortunate breakdown in communications, never reached the Commanding Officer.

Under cover of smoke 'A' & 'B' Coys advanced from the FUP across open ground towards St. HONORINE. The enemy position was penetrated but heavy MMG and artillery fire from SP guns inflicted considerable casualties and it was obvious that a very gallant attempt by these Coys, supported only by very slender artillery and MMG fire, could not succeed. 'A' & 'B' Coys were forced to fall back on LONGUEVAL and the Commanding Officer, who had arrived at hill 30, gave instructions for 'C' Coy to withdraw from that position and concentrate with the remainder of the Bn in the defence of LONGUEVAL.'

So, owing to a series of delays which ultimately deprived the RUR of their heavy artillery and mortar support the attack on St. Honorine was pushed back. War diary entries, essential reading for historians and researchers, leave us with an often cold and factual account of incidents. To grasp an idea of how those facts played out and the effect they had to the infantryman on the ground we have to refer to our witness testimonies.

D-Day Plus One, 11.00hrs

Sam LOWRY:
'On the 7th we had to take two objectives. We took the first one with no trouble at all, fixed bayonets à la '14-18, to me anyway in our particular position it was dead on, but when we went to the second one, St. Honorine, it was a different kettle of fish entirely. We had two platoons up and two platoons in the rear to attack. The four platoon sergeants were WATSON, McALPINE, McCULLY and myself. Watson, McAlpine and McCully were old soldiers, they had been on the Frontier. I was only a kid at 21 or 22 but that was my platoon, and we went in on a frontal attack.

We hit heavy opposition there, I was in one of the rear platoons and I finished up being a forward platoon and under fire. I always remember lying, I don't remember where my platoon commander was, I think he may have been hit and we were pinned down with heavy fire but what annoyed me most was that my haversack was being knocked, as I was lying flat on my belly, by rounds. There was somebody hitting it and he wasn't low enough to hit me. I let a yell out of me to whoever it was in the platoon to stop moving (drawing fire). It was a very old friend of mine who had been with me in many a campaign afterwards, he said 'Sergeant, I'm only trying to get a drink out of my water bottle.' A country man he was, I didn't say anything, but we had to withdraw from that position, we couldn't attack

St. Honorine. The second in command of the battalion said we had to pull back, we couldn't have held the position, all we were doing was getting casualties and nothing in return. We pulled back to a little orchard, and we were shouted at by a little French man who thought we were Germans, and we were running out. What we were doing was running around the yard to get into a better fire position, when he realised this, he stopped shouting at us. They (the Germans) came in and we beat them off, that was it. We were in a sticky position really and we were on the defensive. They were good troops; they were good troops the Germans in those days. It's very easy to say that the commander had underestimated, the commander was in the insidious position that he had his objectives to take. You have to attack with what you have, make do with what you have and that's it.'

For Bill McConnell the events of the 7th June 1944 would resonate long after his return from France and Germany; the attempt to take St. Honorine, the tactics and strategies employed by the senior officers were all ultimately compounded in Bill's memory into the loss of a lifelong friend.

Bill McCONNELL:
'The battalion was ordered by General Gayle to take Longueval. Longueval was one of the pivots of the British army and Longueval was to be held, no matter cost, no matter lives, Longueval was to be held. We done an attack there on the morning of the 7th June then we went up to St. Honorine and we tried to go through there on our frontal attack, there were two companies, 'A' and 'B' Company. We lost a lot that morning, that's where Bobby Stevenson was killed by an 88 millimetre, some were captured and some wounded like Sammy Glass, because we found Sammy Glass's body four days after in a corn field. We had about

20 or 30 missing and some killed you know but we found the graves of some of them buried at Colombelles, where the Germans buried them. We were beaten back out of St. Honorine but we came back to Longueval and held Longueval when the attack was put in on us. Battalion headquarters was cut off for the Germans had surrounded them, but they fought their way out of it and 'D' Company and 'C' Company supported them because 'C' Company was in the Ring Contour and could see what was going on.

Well Bobby Stevenson and I went to school together and were chums together. Bobby went to the first battalion at the same time as I did from the young soldier's battalion the 70th Battalion, Young Soldiers and he joined 'B' Company and he joined the Recce Platoon which was attached to 'A' Company and on the morning of the 6th/7th of June the battalion had been ordered, the CO had been ordered by General Gayle for the battalion, two companies to take St. Honorine as they thought there was no-one there, only a few 'Reichmar' which was the equivalent to a territorial soldier. But they found out afterwards it was the 21st Panzer, all soldiers who had been to Africa who were up against us, the most elite soldiers in the German Army. Now we went in as boys who had never heard an angry shot except in a backfire of a car or on a range, but we went in there as boys against men who were seen as soldiers. We were beaten back but we went back as far as Longueval which wasn't very far just that hedgerow, just down there. (Where the 1st Battalion Memorial is.) Well on the morning of the 7th June we were lying at Longueval and we took up position in line with 'B' Company and we formed up and were supposed to go in at 7 o'clock in the morning, we were supposed to attack but the attack was held up until midday until the naval guns and the Canadian artillery was supporting us was ready. At 12 o'clock we were given the order to advance, 'A' and 'B' Company. 'D' Company was the reserve company at Longueval, 'C' Company in

the ring contour. 'A', 'B', 'C' and 'D'. 'A' and 'B' Company, we did the frontal attack. As we went up to the corn field the corn was up to here, up to the neck on us. As we went up to the corn field there was a little hillock there, as I say it has all changed there entirely, you wouldn't realise that it was the same place. There was a little hillock there and as soon as we got over the top of it to go down into the dip, we seen what we thought was a fence in front of us, but this fence started moving back. We thought we were seeing things. Then the guns started shelling, our guns, in a creeping barrage. And the creeping barrage ended up both them and the Canadians were firing on top of us. Then the Germans started, and we were caught in an arc of fire. We couldn't go forward, we couldn't go back, we couldn't go left, we had to go right and it was across a small wall and in the small wall there was a hole, you know a gap, Captain Martin was on the other side and he brought them all across and when he said run you run but every second one was getting shot as the German snipers were already onto that, to what was going on. But we got most of them out and we all fell back to Longueval. Now it was through our own artillery and the Naval artillery was to give us the creeping barrage, it was to clear the Germans, they didn't, they were clearing us, they killed our people. It was pretty terrible. If I hadn't have got my mind settled in the early hours of the morning of the 7th I would definitely have went away, my mind would definitely have gone. I happened to bring some of my own people out, helped some of my own people out of it. I was a corporal at the time, and I took some of my section out.

But anyway, as they lined up, I was on the right of 'A' Company on the advance. Major Rickcord was the company commander of 'A' Company, and he gave the order to advance as extended order, that's the two companies extended as they went up the field. Bobby Stevenson, he shouted at me, he said 'Bill, I'll see you afterwards'. But

I happened to turn round and there was a shell, an 88 millimetre and he was blown to pieces. Now there wasn't a senior officer near him when this happened but there must be a senior officer present to say he had been killed. There wasn't even his bootlaces left. That's why Bobby Stevenson is named as still missing in action. That's the way it was.

I go there (to the Bayeux Memorial) ... I go there and I lay a cross at the bottom there. I can still see him. Even though it is just a name on the wall. The mind plays games with you and my mind unfortunately is a bit telescopic. I can see things you know that happened years ago. It's sixty years next year. Well, Bobby Stevenson's brother was a sergeant in the Ox and Bucks at that time, 3rd of September when we were coming home, we were climbing up the net to get on the boat at Arromanches. The man beside me was Jim Stevenson and he said to me 'Bill, where's Bobby? Is Bobby on here?' And I said 'What? Bobby was killed' and he said, 'No, he's not.' I said, 'Yes, he is!' So he wasn't even informed and he was part of the 52nd Ox and Bucks. Now he couldn't get home to his father, he said to me 'Could you tell my father if he hasn't already got news?' His father was a road man, a road sweeper at that time at Carnmoney, the bottom of Carnmoney Hill, I went to see him, and he hadn't been told his son was killed. I thought his father would have known, but his father didn't know. It was only after he got onto the War Office that they apologised and said they were sorry that they had despatched a telegram but he didn't get it. I didn't know what to do, Jim wouldn't believe me, his father wouldn't believe me. Eventually he did get word through from the War Office that he was missing, but I said he was killed in this (action). But the father died without knowing any... That was Bobby's family, he had a brother in the regiment. His brother has just died there, just recently, he became a major and a quartermaster in the Ox and Bucks.

I was only 20 when I had to do that. I was 20 when I came

back from France. It's bloody terrible because I didn't want to do it but I knew the family and they knew me. One of them things.'

By 16.00hrs on the 7th June the attack by the 1st RUR on St. Honorine la Chardonerette was effectively over. The men of the 21st Panzer Division counter attacked using self-propelled artillery and mortar fire forcing 'C' Company to withdraw from the 'Ring Contour 30' position and the Riflemen eventually dug into defensive positions around the village on Longueval on the eastern bank of the River Orne. The battalion War Diary recorded the casualties as follows[6]; Lieutenant J.D.A. Boustead and four other ranks killed, Lieutenants O'Hara-Murray, Murphy, Hindson, Dean and H.R. Morgan with 64 other ranks were wounded and Lieutenant Reginald Norman Morgan along with 67 other ranks were recorded as being missing in action. Lieutenant Reginald Morgan had been observed leaving St. Honorine along with his platoon when ordered to withdraw. His body wasn't recovered until 11th July 1944 when the battalion had taken up positions nearby at Le Mesnil[7]. A patrol was sent into the area around the walled orchard at St. Honorine where the battalion was repulsed a month earlier and the 11 marked graves were found in two small plots containing the bodies of those lost in the fighting on the 7th June. The bodies had been buried and marked by the Germans after the battle. A second patrol was sent into the area the following day, 12th July 1944, led by Captain Burke of 'B' Company in an attempt to identify further graves but they were forced to withdraw due to enemy mortar fire.

Those recorded efforts in July 1944 to recover and identify the men missing in action represented just part of a series of ongoing enquiries which continued for the duration of the war and for years after. A dark shadow hung over the nation

6 Ibid.
7 Ibid.

since the days of the Great War and the legacy of the missing, numbering in the hundreds of thousands, those soldiers killed in action but for many different reasons were deprived of the dignity of a grave. The effect on morale of an ever-increasing list of missing among the casualty lists was detrimental to say the least. We have heard how dealing with a missing colleague had impacted on Bill McConnell when at just 20 years of age he was left to explain the unexplainable to the father of Robert Stevenson. The absence of armies filling long lines of trenches of opposing troops and massive artillery barrages to a greater degree decreased the incidents of The Missing considerably but the fluid, mobile combat employed during the 1939 to 1945 war introduced further complications when it came to the marking of the graves of the fallen. There is no doubt much had been learned from 1914–1918 but the possibility of suffering missing casualties remained.

Lists of missing British soldiers were collated at the War Office Casualty Branch, then follow-up enquiries were actioned out to various agencies in an attempt to cover every eventuality whereby a missing soldier may turn up. Fellow soldiers returning from the front for redeployment or recovering in hospitals in England were contacted and interviewed regarding their knowledge of missing men. They were asked to fill out and sign pro-forma questionnaires covering when and where they may have last seen a missing man and whether they were alive, dead, wounded or possibly taken prisoner. Enquiries were then carried out with the International Committee of the Red Cross (ICRC) who, as a neutral organisation were in a position to pass information relating to prisoners of war through diplomatic channels between the various combatting nations. Information was also received, as we have seen, from units on the ground relating to graves found in their areas of operation. Today, many of these records can be found in the National Archives at Kew in London. The statements attached to the questionnaires can give us a little vignette view

of a battle, a moment in time as perceived by the witness at a particular place and in relation to one individual, the missing soldier. Examination of these documents, particularly in larger actions, can give us a more exact idea of how the fortunes of battle turned for the individuals involved.

For the 1st Battalion of The Royal Ulster Rifles the initial missing report following the action on the 7th June 1944 contained the names of 42 men[8]. By July 1945, following the extensive enquiries carried out by the War Office, that list had been reduced considerably to just 6 men: Riflemen W.H. JONES, W.R. MERRELL, J.H. NELSON, Lance Corporal C. O'BRIEN, Rifleman P. MAGUIRE and Bill McConnell's friend Rifleman Robert STEVENSON.

On the 19th July 1945, at the request of the War Office, Corporal P BUCKLEY of 'A' Company made a statement to Lieutenant WATSON who reported what he had been told with regard to the action at St. Honorine as follows:

'I have interviewed Corporal Buckley, and he has given me the following information.

He was told that 7022700 Rfm W.H. Jones and 7047994 Rfm P. Maguire were killed at St. Honorine la Chardonerette approx 5 miles from Caen during an attack made on St. Honorine by 'A' Coy 1st Batt Royal Ulster Rifles.

He is unable to say who gave him this information but thinks it most unlikely that they could be found now as they had very heavy casualties crossing the Rhine.

With regard to L/Cpl C. O'Brien he was told by Rfm Meechan of 'A' Coy 1st Batt R.U.R. that O'Brien lost his leg during the same attack, namely St. Honorine and it happened at about the same position that the two other men were killed.

Buckley said he made enquiries about O'Brien because they lived

---

8 The National Archives, WO 361/585 Royal Ulster Rifles, Missing, North-West Europe.

in the same area at home before the war and were therefore friends.

He thinks that Cpl Simpson of 'A' Coy may be able to give more information, particularly regarding O'Brien because he was there and later taken prisoner. He has since returned to this country and was seen by Buckley on leave some short time ago.'

Following up on the statement made by Corporal Buckley, Corporal Simpson was interviewed on 22 July 1945 and provided the following information:

'I regret that I am unable to give you any information concerning W.R. Merrell, J.H. Nelson, R.J. Stevenson and P. Maguire.

W.H. Jones I last saw when passing through Transit Camp 12A at Limberg. His description is as follows: small, medium build, age about 22 years, lives in North of England and was in 10 Platoon in 'A' Coy.

C. O'Brien was wounded at the top of his right leg and I last saw him in a corn field at St. Honorine. His description: Short and stout, age about 23 years, lives in Southern Ireland, probably Dublin and was L/Cpl in my section, 10 Platoon, 'A' Coy.'

It later transcribed that an administrative mistake had been made with regards to Rifleman W.M. Jones whose name should have been recorded as William Henry JOHNS. Johns had been evacuated to a dressing station at Ranville on 7th June and subsequently died of his wounds. He was initially buried close to the original RUR Headquarters position at Bas De Ranville farm. His grave was exhumed and he was finally laid to rest at Ranville Military Cemetery on 20th July 1944.

Rifleman Walter Richard Merrell's body was also buried at Ranville Military Cemetery. The first record of a grave having been identified as his, is dated January 1955. There are no further details available relating to how his grave was found but it is likely that he was also fatally wounded and evacuated to Ranville for

treatment where he later died of his wounds.

On the 27th July 1944 Corporal W. CARLISLE was interviewed and asked of his knowledge of any of the men on the 7th June list. With regards to Rifleman Nelson, he made the following statement:

'Rfm Nelson was in my section and reached the wall in the village of St. Honorine. From this wall we had eventually to withdraw. I did not see Rfm Nelson after this point.'

His statement, although minimal in content was of assistance in identifying one of the bodies previously buried by the Germans at the area of the wall at St. Honorine and recovered on 17th July 1945 that were marked originally with only a partial service number of 5185. Rifleman Nelson's full service number was 6985185. He was reburied along with six other riflemen whose graves were found in the same area, at Ranville Military Cemetery.

From the scant account available, which to a certain extent is hearsay, all we know about Rifleman Patrick MAGUIRE and Lance Corporal Charles O'BRIEN is that they lost their lives in action in the corn field approaching the perimeter wall surrounding the village of St. Honorine La Chardonerette possibly in the same area where Bill McConnell found the body of his friend Samuel GLASS. In the case of Charles O'Brien, we can say with a degree of certainty that he was seriously wounded having possibly lost a leg. It may have been the case that he was tended to by German medics and died shortly afterwards in a different location to the areas where the remaining bodies were found or that he and Patrick Maguire both suffered a similar fate to that of Robert Stevenson and that ultimately there simply was nothing left to find.

Their names join that of Rifleman Woodburn and to this day remain on the list of those who are still missing in action.

The men of the 2nd Battalion also found themselves confronted

by a village surrounded by a wall. The enemy behind that wall west of the Orne unfortunately played by different rules when it came to the treatment of wounded and the burial of the fallen.

5

D-Day Plus One: West of the Orne

Cambes Wood

D-Day Plus One, 00.00hrs
Périers-sur-le-Dan

After taking a number of casualties in the area of The Orchard at Hermanville-sur-Mer, mainly due to enemy sniping activities the men of the 2nd battalion, Royal Ulster Rifles made their way in a southeasterly direction inland to a ridge dominated by a farm at Périers-sur-le-Dan where they came to halt at nightfall. Unsure as to whether they were to move on immediately or not, rather than dig in as per their training the men bivouacked in the open, some simply lay in fields and others taking cover from in a small, wooded area adjacent to the farm buildings. In a similar way to their 1st Battalion colleagues east of the River Orne the men found that their immediate enemy was in their own minds as darkness and apprehension played games in their imagination. Occasionally however those feelings of doubt were well-founded.

Hamilton LAWRENCE:
'The Battalion re-grouped in a field, we couldn't get moving, we were supposed to carry on, but we just stopped on the first night. We didn't get digging in at all there, we just

stayed there in the field, any place that you could get for shelter was just there, it wasn't in the woods, it was out in the open at that time and we stayed out there the whole night. We were soaking wet and that's where we regrouped to go into Cambes Wood. I felt terrible – scared – not knowing what was going to happen or what we were going to do the next day. We had no rations; no food and what compound rations you had was all destroyed with the water. They brought some food to us the next morning, we managed to get something before we did the attack. Nobody was feeling any good then. Miserable, really miserable, it wasn't too bad when the sun was coming up but through the night, we didn't know who was there because we didn't know who got off the (landing) craft. All you knew was your own section and your own platoon because the battalion headquarters had a space of their own where the company runners reported. You wanted to see who was there and who was missing, nobody knew who was in charge really. During the night you seen nothing (you were) just lying there, talking a wee bit. It was frightening when you didn't know anybody to talk to. We couldn't dig in; we never got a chance to dig in because we were told we were going to move again.

It was miserable. All you seen was Verey Lights, the sky lit up, planes going over, you could still hear the roar of the planes going over and the ships at sea firing all their guns, the warships and all their support firing all of their guns. That's all you seen the whole night long, firing back and forward. You were worrying about one of them (shells) dropping on you because they were dropping near hand you know, dropping near the beach – the enemy ones were – and ours were dropping just in front of us as well.'

Stanley BURROWS:
'The first night we spent in an apple orchard, and I can remember well my first night sleeping in a trench in the field of battle, we were lying there, and I had another lad

with me called Jim, he was in the trench along with me. You dug a trench in this war, not like the First World War, they were just wee trenches about the size of a grave, you dug it according to your size, if you were tall, you had a step deeper than I had on my side of the trench. The two of us were sitting there and when darkness comes and you're tired and you're weary and you're staring into the dark, the more you stare into it the more you imagine you see something moving.

It was my turn to take a wee rest and I was sitting in the bottom of the trench and my chum Jim kept saying 'There's something moving out there'. I stood up and looked out and I could see nothing. I said 'Jim, look, there's nothing out there, you're tired and you're only imagining things, it might be sheep, it might be anything.' The second time he shouted 'Look, there it is!'. I jumped up and there was a shadow of this man walking in the dark. Lance Corporal White shouted out 'Leave him to me Stanley, cover me.' I brought up the Bren gun, covered the man and as Lance Corporal White got out to go forward to the man, all of a sudden two shots fired out. It hit this man, we saw later, in the groin but he was lying shouting 'Mercy kamarad! Mercy kamarad!' We advanced forward, I was covering with the gun, my officer Lieutenant Welsh and Lance Corporal White went forward. Lance Corporal White lifted his rifle, his gun and was going to shoot him, Lieutenant Walsh said 'No, we want none of that.' He had already been in Italy and fought there. He said. 'We will have none of that.' White said to him 'They've killed my brother and I've no respect for any of them.' Nevertheless, they didn't harm him, but the interpreters came up quick to try to speak to him in German to find any information they could out of him.

That was my first night there in the trench with my chum. There was shelling throughout the night, but I don't think there were any of us injured for the rest of the night.'

Richard KEEGAN:
'There was a bit of sniping went on in The Orchard, this fella, if you moved at all he had a clear vision of what was going on and you more or less had to keep your head down. The boys that were dug in further round where the trees were, some of them plugged him. Whenever it came to the bit he didn't fall out of the tree whenever he was hit – he'd himself strapped in and he had his weapon strapped in, that was in case he fell asleep that he wouldn't fall out of the tree. He was there for the night to do the job. A whole lot of fellas were hit (by snipers) and they all seemed to be hit in the head because their head was just that wee bit too far up and he got the snapshot in. Most of them got out of there in one piece and up to where we dug in for the night. There were trees all around a farmhouse and we were dug in, the company. I don't know where the other companies dug in. All we were looking for was something to eat, when were we going to get a feed? Ritchie the cook got the thing going for us and when we got something to eat, we were all right.

I thought I was doing a really smart thing on the boat, I put a pair of socks in my mess tin because when we were doing the landings in Scotland your feet were always soaking, I said 'I'll have a pair of dry socks with me', so whenever we dug in for the night we always dug a trench for the pair of us and we always dug a hole in the side wall of the trench and we were able to make a drop of tea in that as we had the equipment to do that – our hard tack as they called it. I took my mess tin out and had to take my socks out and they were wringing wet, so I had no need to change my socks and I just hung out the ones that I had on over the back of the trench to dry out. We made ourselves a tin of soup. We were soaked and still had to carry on.

We had a talk, we were going to attack, it wasn't Cambes Wood then, it was whatever the (code) name was for it. The officers had the talk with the company commander who had a talk with the platoon officers. The next morning

Jimmy PEDLOW got out of his trench to light a butt and the first shell came over and landed among us. He got it in the neck and that was the first casualty that I really seen.'

Medical Sergeant DRUMGOOLE made an entry in his casualty record which corresponds to the incident involving Jimmy Pedlow; the entry, which was the first made on the 7th June 1944 simply states '7021772 Rfm Pedlow 'D' Shrapnel Neck Ridge'. The 'Ridge' being the location of the battalion at that time on the ridge at Périers-sur-le-Dan. Before the day passed sixty-five more entries were made in his book.

The 2nd RUR Battalion War Diary[1] outlined the basic orders for the taking of the village of Cambes:

'The battalion was ordered to move in a South Westerly direction to capture Cambes, a small village thickly wooded, approximately six miles inland from the coast. The Battalion moved via Le Mesnil with 'D' Company, commanded by Captain J.R.StL. Aldworth as vanguard. It was believed that Cambes was lightly held, but as the woods surrounding it were themselves surrounded by walls some ten feet high, it was not possible to observe the enemy's dispositions. 'D' Company was ordered to proceed forward and capture Cambes with the rest of the Battalion closely following in reserve.'

So, owing to the topography of the village with thick woods and surrounding walls, a detailed reconnaissance could not be carried out.

'D' Company moved off from the attack start line at 17.00hrs on the 7th June 1944. At this precise time an intelligence summary was recorded in the War Diary of the Headquarters of the 6th Airborne Division. Four German prisoners had been captured in the Ranville area and were found to have belonged to the 12 SS Panzer Division 'Hitlerjugend'. After interrogation it was

1 The National Archives, WO 171/1384, War Diary, 2nd Royal Ulster Rifles.

discovered that they had been stragglers from their battalion's reconnaissance unit who stated that they had been ordered to move west through Caen in preparation for a counterattack on the Allied beachheads. The prisoners had in fact taken a wrong turn in Caen and found themselves on the eastern side of the river Orne by mistake. An assessment of this intelligence was made and recorded as follows:

'It appears that elements of 21 Panzer Division have been given the role of containing the Airborne Forces east of the Orne whilst 12 SS Panzer Division Hitlerjugend passes through Caen or south of Caen to attack the allied beachheads. On D+2 a continuancy of these attacks must be expected whilst 12 SS Panzer Division moves west of Caen.'[2]

Whereby the initial part of this assessment was correct, elements of the 21st Panzer Division had indeed been given the role of containing the Airborne assault east of the Orne, the remainder was not what played out on the ground. The 12 SS 'Hitlerjugend', under the command of Standartenführer Kurt MEYER had moved west and north from Caen maintaining elements of the 21st Panzer Division on their right flank and were ready to go into action on 7th June, not D-Day Plus Two as anticipated. Two battalions of the 12 SS Division's 25th Panzer-grenadier Regiment had taken up position right in front of the 2nd Royal Ulster Rifles as described by Obersturmbannführer Hubert MEYER[3] (No relation to Kurt Meyer):

'At 15.00hrs Standartenführer Meyer (Kurt) had ordered the I and II battalion to also be ready for the attack as soon as the respective

---

2   The National Archives, WO223/15, Staff College Camberley 1947 Course Notes, D-Day + War Diary HQ 6 A/B Div 6 – 12 June 1944.
3   Hubert Meyer, 'The 12th SS Vol. One – The History of the Hitler Youth Panzer Division' J.J. Fedorowicz Publishing Inc. 1994, Stockpole Books editions 2005, 2021.

(1) Rifleman Edmund James (Jim) Whitehorn, 2nd Battalion Royal Ulster Rifles, killed in action on board the SS *Sambut*, 6th June 1944. The note 'To Doll' on the photograph relates to the affectionate name he used for his wife Emmie. *(Courtesy of Whitehorn/Fuller family)*

(2) Doreen Fuller at the section of the Normandy Memorial which bears her father Jim Whitehorn's name, September 2023. *(Courtesy of S.J. Wright)*

(3) Doreen Fuller and family. *(Courtesy of S.J. Wright)*

(4) SS *Sambut* ablaze off Goodwin Sands, 6th June 1944. (*From I.W.M. footage*)

(5) Horsa Glider, showing the running wheels used for take-off and then jettisoned and the central skid used for landing.

(6) Horsa Glider, front-on view of cockpit.

(7) Horsa Glider view of interior and seating. (Images 5–7 were taken at the reconstructed glider exhibit on display at The Pegasus Bridge Museum.)

(8) View of the original Pegasus Bridge now moved and displayed as an exhibit within the grounds of the Pegasus Bridge Museum, Normandy.

(9) View of the interior of an original Horsa Glider used in the invasion and recovered for display at the Pegasus Bridge Museum. This fuselage section appears to have been part of a glider configured to carry a Jeep and trailer.

(10) View looking towards the village of Cambes en Plaine from the start line of the attack on the 7th June 1944 close to the village of Anisy.

(11) Cambes railway halt and the view along the road which was the railway line in 1944, and which ran parallel to the wall around the village.

(12) The church at Cambes which marked the final objective of the 9th June 1944 attack. Today murals on a building nearby mark the liberation of the village by the 2nd RUR.

(13) The church and church tower beside Ranville War Cemetery, Ranville, Normandy.

(14) The grave of the unknown German sniper 'taken down' by Bill McConnell on the 7th June 1944. Ranville Churchyard Cemetery, Ranville, Normandy.

(15) Rifleman Hamilton Lawrence (circled in red) photographed attending the briefing given at Droxford by General Montgomery on 19th May 1944. *(I.W.M., War Office Collection, H38647)*

(16) 'The way to Paris', a photograph taken after the liberation of Caen in July 1944, which shows Lt. Cyril Rand (right) referred to in the text. *(Getty Images, Bettmann Collection, U999239INP)*

(17) Photograph of George Horner, taken November 2023.

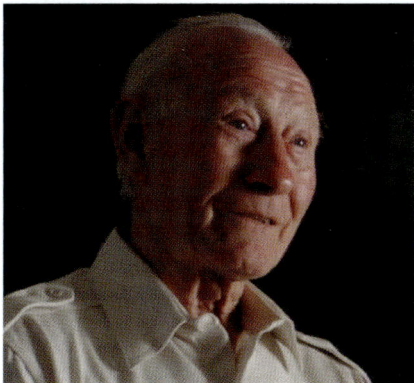

Hamilton 'Hammy' Lawrence,
2nd Battalion Royal Ulster Rifles from
Belfast.

James 'Jimmy' Bowden, 591 (Antrim)
Parachute Squadron, Royal Engineers
from Whiteabbey, County Antrim.

Bill McConnell, 1st (Airborne)
Battalion Royal Ulster Rifles from
Belfast.

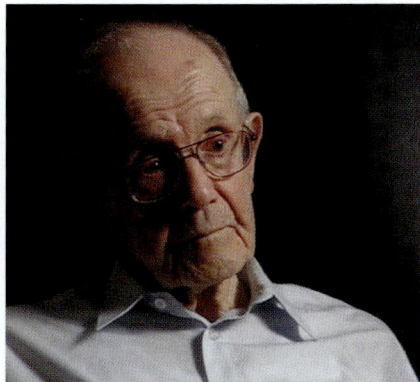

Samuel 'Sam' Lowry, 1st (Airborne)
Battalion Royal Ulster Rifles from
Carrickfergus, County Antrim.

Richard Keegan, 2nd Battalion Royal Ulster Rifles, from Lurgan, County Armagh.

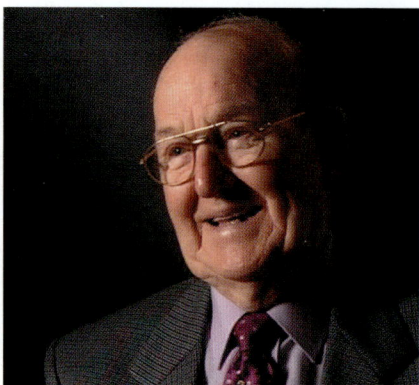

Stanley Burrows, 2nd Battalion Royal Ulster Rifles from Belfast.

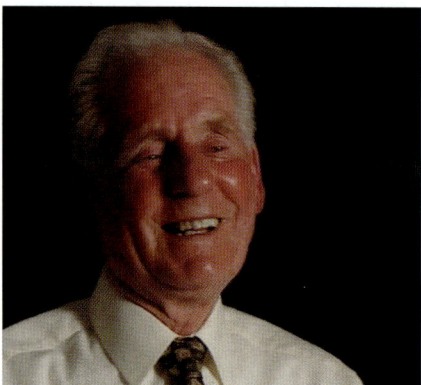

Martin Vance, 1st (Airborne) Battalion Royal Ulster Rifles from Belfast.

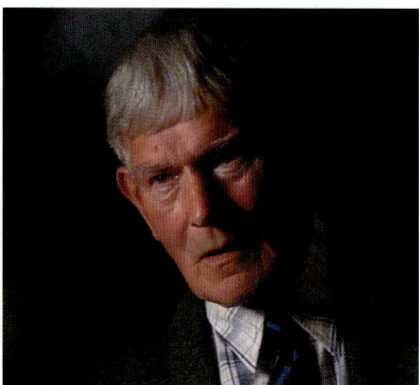

Robert Loughlin, 1st (Airborne) Battalion Royal Ulster Rifles from Ballyclare, County Antrim.

(18) *Images courtesy of DoubleBand Films.*

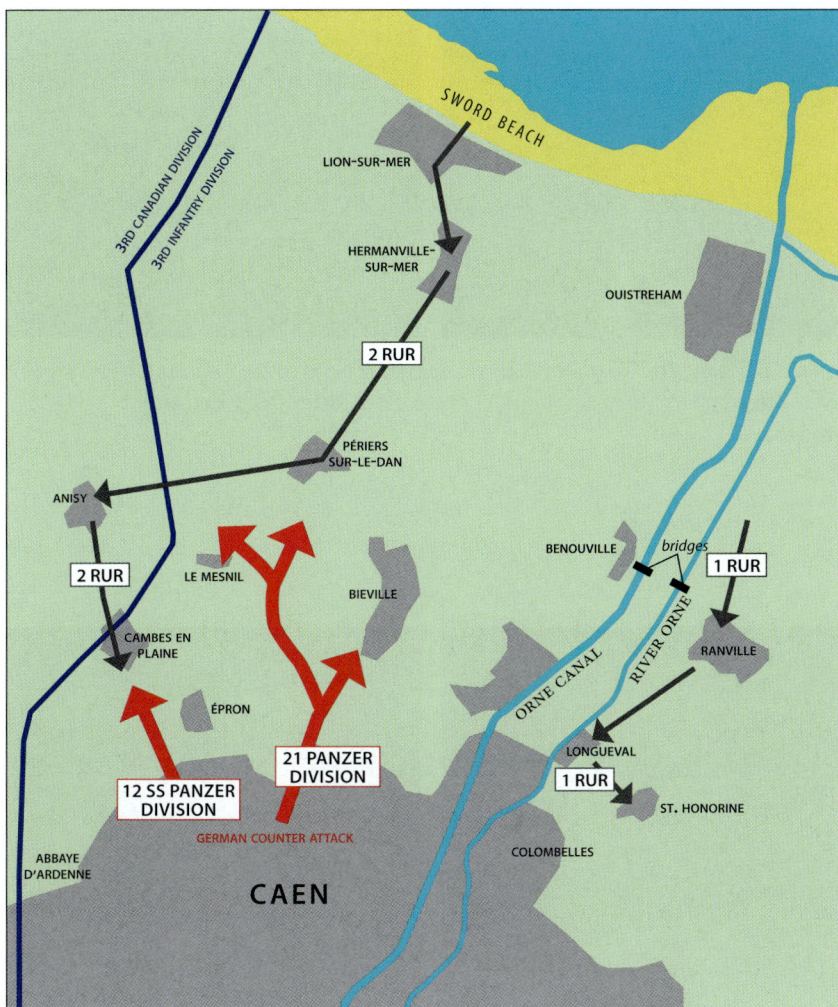

(19) Map showing approach to Caen, East and West of the River Orne.

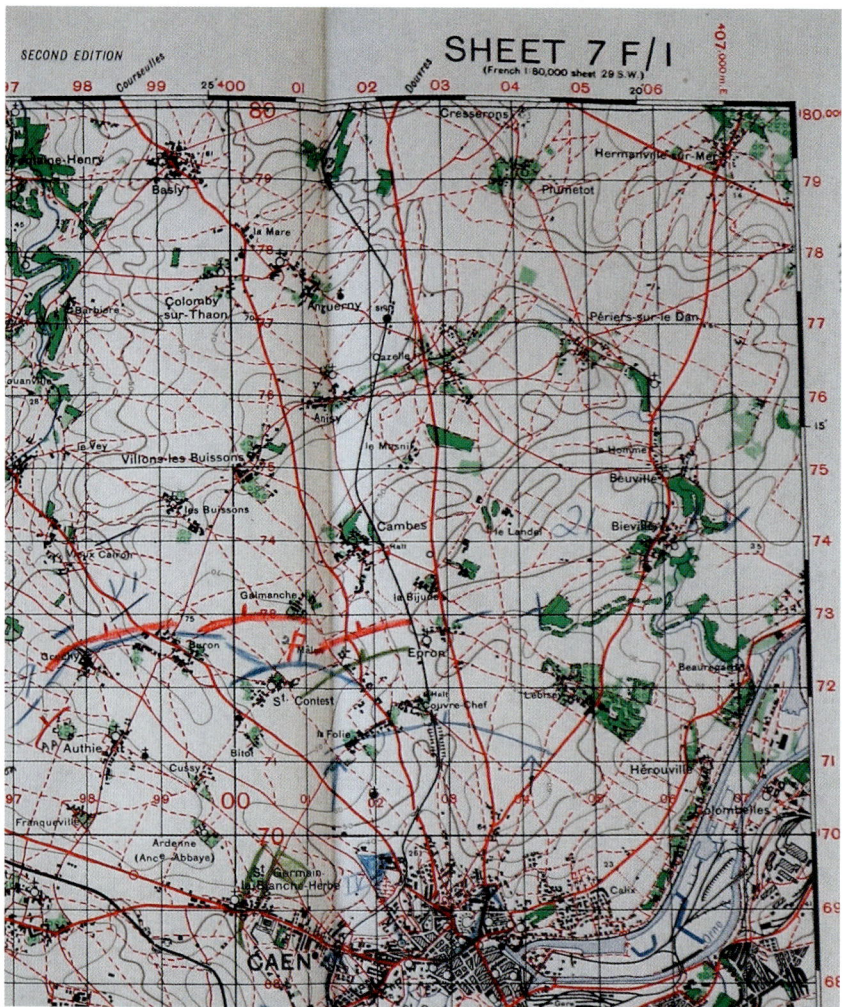

(20) Section of map Sheet 7F/1 which was annotated by SS General Kurt Meyer during an interview in relation to war crimes. He marked the positions of his three 12th SS Panzergrenadier battalions on the 7th June 1944 in red to the south of Cambes, 1st Battalion on right, 2nd Battalion centre and 3rd Battalion left. He also marked in blue the position of the 21st Panzer Division to the east on the map between Cambes-en-Plaine and Bieville.
(The National Archives, TS 26/856 Supplementary Report of SHAEF – Shooting of allied Prisoners of war by 12th SS Panzer Division.)

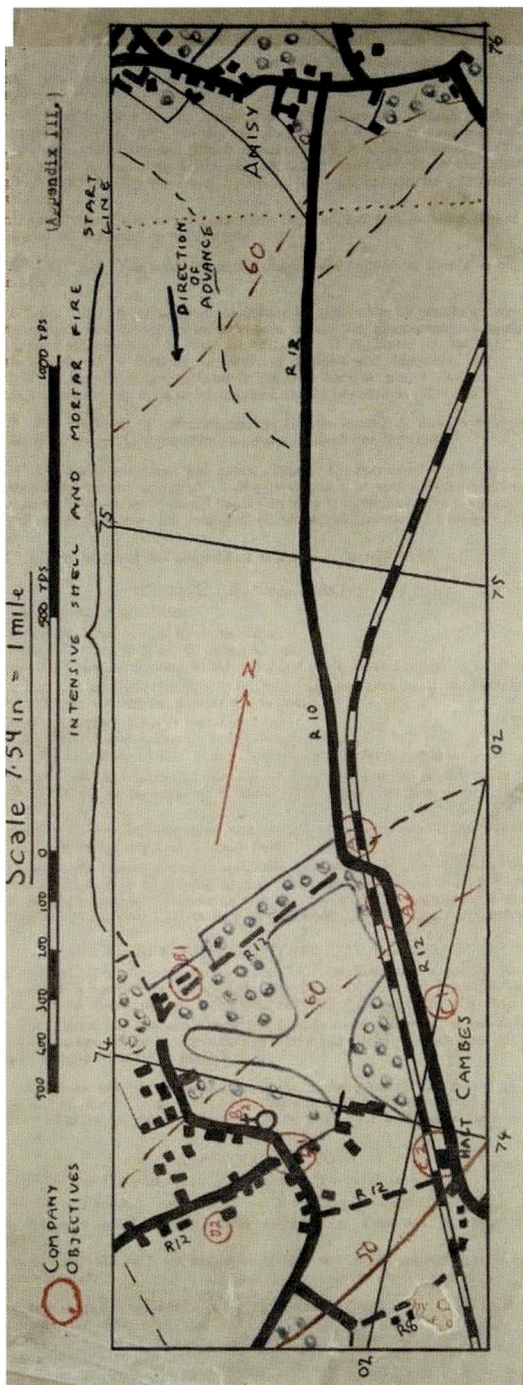

(21) Map showing company objectives 2nd RUR for Battle of Cambes on 9th June 1944. Direction of attack was North to South, top to bottom on this page. (*The National Archives, WO 171/1384, War Diary, 2nd Royal Ulster Rifles.*)

battalion on the left had reached the same line. The II Battalion (on the left flank) did not have any enemy directly in front of it... The right wing (of the I Battalion) bore the brunt of the 2nd Royal Ulster Regiment and the supporting tanks of the East Riding Yeomanry, attacking from Le Mesnil towards Cambes.'

In the space of just a few hours the advancing 12th SS Panzer Division had been able to halt and consolidate at the village of Cambes. A deadly trap was set for the men of the 2nd Royal Ulster Rifles which was sprung by the advancing 'D' Company.

D-Day Plus One, Cambes Woods, 17.00hrs

Hamilton LAWRENCE:

'On the 7th we got the orders that we were going to move and attack Cambes, they gave the orders as to where we were going to go and they said 'D' Company is going to be the advance company to take Cambes, that's your objective, to take Cambes Wood. So, we got out of the wood into the open, once we got into the open there was a bit of a road and the road encircled Cambes and also a wood. We got through the wood all right and out onto a main road to the open (looking) actually into the village itself and we could see the church and all there. We got in there and as soon as we got out of the wood it started. What happened, I got out with my section and my section got across the road, got over the hedge up onto the open country to see what it was like there. So, when I got there I had a mortar and two men with me, I got across and got into a field and we seen this tank coming down the road around the corner. He stopped at the corner and looked around; he didn't see anybody in the wood. I got over the road and I was looking round for my mate for the ammunition for the 2-inch mortar and he was on the other side, back in the woods again. He never got across – when he seen the tank, they said stop there. I

couldn't get back again, we had to wait until the tank went right back round in a circle and went back again. Then they started, they must have seen us from the church outpost, and they opened fire. There was no way we could have got across and we had to go back again.'

Stanley BURROWS:

'When we advanced across there it was very heavy corn, it was thick, so we were over waist deep in corn. When a man was hit and fell in that corn you couldn't just see where he was. 'A' Company was on reserve, we were on the right flank and as we were coming up the road in reserve four German aircraft came down on us and they machine gunned right up the centre of the road. Every one of us dived quickly to each side of the road, to the ditch. That road was absolutely cut to pieces, you could see it tearing up the middle but not one of us was hit. We came out of it and I don't know how. You could actually see when you looked up that they were that close above you you could see the pilots sitting in their seats. We dived in to the one side and we weren't hit then.

We covered the right flank; I was on the right hand side with a Bren gun with a fellow with me called Welsh. He was lying beside me, and this tank was cutting the corn to pieces. I think they were trying to search out anybody who was lying there, he kept whispering in my ear 'Stanley, shoot!' And I kept whispering back 'Quiet!'. Well, he went quiet and after a while the firing stopped. He said to me 'Stanley, I don't mind telling you, I said a wee prayer there.' I said, 'I'll tell you something I said more prayers there than the Padre has said all his life!' He said to me 'Why did you not fire?' I said 'If I had've fired a Bren gun at a Tiger tank it would have been like peas coming off a wall from a peashooter. You and I wouldn't have been here now if I had have fired, they would have known where you and me were.' When I stood up we had a bit of a laugh because I felt my trousers very wet at my rear end. I thought that in

the excitement I had wet myself, I put my hand down and felt that my trousers were soaking and when we looked my water bottle had been hit by a wee bit of shrapnel and the water was running out round my rear end so I'm glad to say I didn't wet myself. It was a bit of an experience lying there in that long corn.'

Richard KEEGAN:

'Whenever we moved off on the 7th to make the first attack on Cambes Wood we were walking along this road, a narrow road, and there was shelling going on and we were very fortunate that there was none landing on the road. We came to this crossroads and there were four high banks and a shell hole to the right of the road and a motorbike was sitting there and the fellow on it and he was as dead as a doornail. There wasn't a spot of blood on him that I could see, and we just walked on. The motorbike was still ticking over. He must have stopped at the crossroads to do a bit of directing whenever the shell landed and blew him onto the bank.

Whenever we got up to the place where we started the attack on Cambes Wood there was this bit of a hedge and a bit of a bank at the road in front of the corn field. There was a big house on the right and at that time I'll swear to this day that there were nuns out working in the garden. There were gaps in the hedge, and you went through them into the corn field and down the corn field. We all lined up and we were told we were attacking, and we could see a hedge, it must have been about 1500 yards across that field. There was shelling and mortaring going on, but we managed to get over it and whenever we came to the first hedge there was a road on the other side of the hedge with a wee railway line running along it. I was wondering if that was for bringing stuff from the farms into the town. Stanley (Burrows) didn't remember that railway line. But anyway, whenever we got across it there was a wall ten feet high and a gap in it just on the corner. The Germans were supposed

to be there and that was the first attack we were making on the way to Caen. Whenever we approached it you couldn't see the wall on account of the hedge on the side of the road. Then, whenever you got across the road there was another bit of a hedge and then you saw the wall, and it was ten feet high. You had no chance of getting over that, no matter whether you were a commando or what you were. The gap in the wall was then at the corner. The wall that was around the wood is away now, but the gap will always be in my mind, the thing that always hits me is 'Will you come into my parlour said the spider to the fly' because it just looked like an invitation in, but you weren't going to get out. We went in. Whenever we went in, we went left and the Company Commander Mr. Greene led us through. Captain Montgomery led the other ones straight on. I got three quarters way, maybe more and we just got pinned down. I actually saw a German soldier leave the farmhouse, that's what was on the left, and he ran down the wood and across the bottom to a machine gun post that was there. Whether he was an officer or whether he was just an ordinary ranker I don't know but we couldn't have hit him because you were just firing into trees. Whenever you got into the woods you were just met with just tree after tree, you were more or less dodging around the trees to move along, whenever you got down you were crawling round them. We got in about a good three quarters of the way into that wood on the left and I would say that Captain Montgomery and his squad got near enough the same (distance) but a machine gun in front opened up and a machine gun to the left opened up along with shelling. That's when Mr. Greene told me 'Go back and see Captain Montgomery and tell him we are pinned down and we're going to get back out again'. I went round the whole cut to Captain Montgomery and told him, he said 'I was thinking the same thing, right boys, out!' They happened to be in a position that they were able to get out before us.

In that wood the Germans were very crafty, they had trip wires and personnel mines, and all tied up in the trees so whether any of the boys had tripped any of them and that's how they were wounded I don't know but there were some wounded anyway, and they were left there. Whenever I came back, I was told to tell Captain Montgomery that Major Aldworth had been killed, I told him in the message and came back again to Mr. Greene, he said 'That's all right, pull out.' So, we all crawled round the trees and out again. Whenever it came to pulling out, we couldn't bring the wounded because we couldn't drag them around trees as close as that. About twenty yards from the trees there was high grass, and you didn't know what was in it. There was a few left wounded, you couldn't have dragged them out the trees were that close together, you would only have done them harm and they were left for the Germans to look after but the Germans, according to Stanley (Burrows), they found them (the wounded) all dead, shot.

I didn't see any panicking or anything like that. I had a few shots all right but whether I done any damage I couldn't tell you. I can remember to the clergymen, they were up with us and they were giving the rites to the fellows and praying for the fellows that went down, one of them had a revolver, I said (to him) 'A man of the cloth with a revolver?' He said 'I would rather it was him in heaven first before me!' He was willing to fight too, he had his revolver and they were up with us right in the leading line. We pulled out and moved back to Anisy and dug in there for the night, a bit of sniping went on there too.'

According to German accounts of the attack on Cambes the result could have been much worse. The RUR action combined with communication difficulties had meant that artillery and tank support could not be brought effectively onto the Cambes area and the 21st Panzer Division on the German right flank had not been in place on time for the attack.

Hubert MEYER, 12th SS Panzer Division 'Hitlerjugend'[4]:
'The I Battalion (25th Panzer-grenadier) could not pursue this retreat. The enemy covered the small, wooded area with strong barrages from artillery and mortars. The advanced observer of 7 Batterie (artillery) which depended on cooperation with I Battalion, was killed. His radio was destroyed preventing further support from German artillery. German Panzers had been rendered inactive. The neighbour on the right, units of the Panzerregiment 22 of the 21 Panzerdivision had not been assembled so that the right flank of the battalion remained open. Under these circumstances, Sturmbannfuhrer (Major) Waldmüller decided to halt the attack, disengage from the enemy and to take up defensive positions on the southern edge of Cambes.'

At the day's end on the 7th June 1944 Sergeant James DRUMGOOLE recorded the details of the casualties sustained during the attack on Cambes Wood[5]. Twenty-six men were recorded as being injured by shrapnel, these from the support companies as well as from the attacking 'D' Company as the Germans directed mortar and artillery fire around Anisy and the wood where the RUR Battalion reserves were positioned. Nine men suffered gunshot wounds including Lieutenant Greene or 'Mr. Greene' as Richard Keegan had respectfully referred to him as in his accounts. Lieutenant Greene suffered gunshot wounds to his back and chest. A total of twenty men were recorded by him as killed, two of them were part of Sgt Drumgoole's own medical team, Riflemen Henry VALENTINE from Harringay in London and Michael MICHAELIDES from Kennington, London who were stretcher-bearers. Of the remaining eighteen entries seventeen of those recorded as being killed were all men from Richard Keegan's 'D' Company and included Major John

---

4 Ibid.
5 James Drumgoole Papers, '2nd Bn Casualties, D-Day' Royal Ulster Rifles Museum, Bedford Street, Belfast.

ALDWORTH the company commander. Four men were recorded as 'missing' after the engagement.

In his humble and 'matter of fact' manner Richard Keegan described his own actions that day in carrying the messages between Lieutenant Greene and Captain Montgomery under fire within the wood. The fact remains that if he had not succeeded in this task, and the men from 'D' Company had remained in the wood any longer, pitted as they were against a battalion of the 12th SS in well prepared positions, their casualty figures would undoubtedly have been much higher.

Stanley BURROWS:

"'D' Company were told that they were going to advance and take out Cambes Woods. Now Cambes Woods was two large woods surrounded by a ten-foot wall. We had no scaling gear; we were told nothing about climbing over walls or anything and when they did a reconnaissance of it they couldn't see very well to see what was inside or what was happening so they didn't know really what they were up against. They thought it was lightly held and they ordered 'D' Company to take the woods. They had to retreat leaving a lot of their dead behind, their Company Commander was killed and some of our own lads, four of them, were wounded and left behind in that wood when they retreated out.'

For Richard Keegan, the battalion runner in 'D' Company, as he returned with the remnants of his company to dig in again at Anisy his thoughts were with those who did not return, either killed in action or left wounded behind the wall at Cambes. Richard thought of the man who checked his watch and told him the time as they were about to land at Sword Beach, just over 24 hours later that man was dead.

Richard KEEGAN:

'The one who stands out is the platoon corporal, Johnny KOHLER. He was a Londoner and we got on the very best, he was no dogmatic sort of a man. It must have been a sniper got him, but he was killed on the 7th of June. Johnny, he was a married man, and he thought an awful lot of his wife and he talked an awful lot of his wife, he seemed to be a good family man. He was a right fellow, whenever you were on parade you stood to attention and 'corporalled' him, whenever you came off the parade ground and into the barrack room I'd say, 'Are you going out for a drink tonight John?' He'd reply 'I think I will.' We would have gone out and had a jar or two. He was a good guy; he was one of the best.

Sometimes I feel that it's a thing that should never have happened.'

By midnight on D-Day Plus One both battalions of the Royal Ulster Rifles found themselves in similar circumstances but in different locations astride the River Orne. They now knew their enemies.

6

D-Day Plus Two:
Longueval and Le Mesnil

Following the withdrawal from St. Honorine the men of the 1st Battalion dug in at Longueval and fought off counterattacks made by the Germans in the hope of taking advantage of the situation. Their positions were put under mortar and artillery fire from at least one German self-propelled gun in the area. The Battalion Headquarters was forced to move from the edge of the village facing St. Honorine to a safer building close to the east bank of the River Orne, which was convenient to a relatively secure resupply route from Ranville along a towpath at the edge of the canal. The steep bank and slope leading down to the river from where the HQ was sited meant that it was difficult for enemy artillery to range onto their positions in the area, so it was deemed to be relatively safe. Before long, in the early afternoon the Battalion was subjected to a vicious artillery barrage from an unexpected quarter, the unfortunate consequence of German sniper activity in the area.

D-Day Plus Two, 15.15hrs

Robert LOUGHLIN:
'There were trees beside the river and trees in at the back of a big house, an old house, we weren't long there a couple of

days, and I went up the stairs, I was going to go up and pull a slate off inside to look out. I wasn't up the stairs two minutes until I heard a terrible bang – there was an explosion. I looked round and I couldn't get back down the stairs. I had to jump over the top of the wall, the brick and things. There was a big hole in the wall. I went down and looked round the corner, I thought, *what was I was going to see?*

Sergeant CHARLES and Ginger BOYD two of my best friends were looking after an anti-tank gun at the corner of the house. I'll never forget it, they were at their gun just at the corner of the house, they got the full blast. There was a wood, and an officer came down the side of the wood, I didn't know if he was 'C' Company or not, I couldn't tell you, but I knew there was something wrong when he had a white hanky. He said to me 'Come on.' I said 'Sir, I can't go and leave these two lads. I have two friends here.' There were a whole lot more down below (wounded) I didn't feel like going either to tell you the truth. Away he went and as he got up to run, he held the hanky up high to get them to stop firing any more. He went over the Orne and he put the hanky up and ran on to get the firing stopped.

A sniper had shot some of them, some of our friends over on the other side of the river, and they retaliated. They thought that we were the Germans and whether they knew that there were British there or not, I don't know. There were a whole lot killed but they got the sniper, a fellow came up and told me he had got the sniper, but as I told him, 'Just too late.' They shifted Sergeant Charles and Rifleman Boyd down below to the Headquarters then they took them that night in Jeeps to the shore to get them to England. It was the Canadians, but they didn't know. I would stand by that. It was desperate, they had some injuries I can tell you and dead. I thought it was terrible, I thought it was terrible.

That officer could have got the M.C., the Military Cross, what did I get? Dust! It was a terrible thing, it's one thing when your enemy wounds you and kills you, but when it

comes to some other regiment, they might have had a bit of gumption.'

Sam LOWRY:
'We were on the flank, and somebody had been shooting at the troops on the other side who were seaborne Canadians. They promptly replied by shelling us, a captain swam the River Orne to tell the Canadians who we were to get the shelling stopped and that was that, it was a strange position to be in. The Canadians thought that we were Germans because we were isolated really. The Canadians wasted no time, I'm not sure if they caused any casualties amongst us.'

The incident described by both Sam Lowry and Robert Loughlin was an unfortunate one to say the least. Five men were killed as a result with a further nine wounded, with one man, Rifleman Edward PAYNE, later dying of his wounds. Rifleman BOYD was one of those wounded and evacuated to the Casualty Clearing Station at Ranville by Jeep using the secure towpath route. Lance Sergeant Allen CHARLES was less fortunate and was one of the five men killed outright in the incident along with Corporal Stuart RAYNHAM, Lance Corporal Henry GREER, Rifleman Arthur STARR and Rifleman Patrick MULLINS. Those killed were buried close to the Battalion Headquarters in the grounds of the home of Monsieur Davoisne whose garage had been set up as a temporary morgue. Their bodies were exhumed in January 1945 and laid to rest together in Ranville Military Cemetery.

The officer who Robert Loughlin had seen waving the white handkerchief was Captain R. RIGBY. Captain Rigby had suspected that the shelling and subsequent direct hit on the battalion anti-tank crew had come from the allied side of the river. He confirmed this by finding a nosecone from one of the exploded shells which confirmed that it was British or allied projectile. Captain Rigby then swam across both the River Orne and parallel Orne Canal

and found the artillery officer, a Canadian Major, and made him cease firing the artillery. Captain Rigby then swam back across the canal and river, narrowly escaping capture and eventually reported to Battalion Headquarters at 18.25hrs; an entry was recorded in the Battalion War Diary[1] as follows:

'*Captain Rigby arrived at Bn.H.Q. and stated that the shelling of the Bn. Area during the afternoon had been by a British unit on far side of river. He had swum river and canal in an endeavour to stop them and had narrowly escaped capture by enemy. He subsequently recrossed the river and canal and reported back in very damp pants and vest.*'

Bill McCONNELL recounted the incident years later with slight differences in the initial sequence of events, he was clear about the result of the officer crossing the river:

'He (the officer) went down to the Canadian artillery and grabbed the Major by the throat and told him to 'Stop now!' As he was killing the Ulster Rifles. There was no F.O. (forward observation) forward post, they were just firing indiscriminately.

Most of the fighting that we did was fighting patrols, we didn't fight as a battalion as such, battalion fighting. We fought as fighting patrols as a platoon going out, or a section going out, something like that and meeting the enemy at very close range, I would say it was all from about 500 yards or 300 yards. We could see them, and they could see us but there was no hand to hand because we couldn't afford to get any closer except when we did an ambush.'

The 1st Battalion set about consolidating their positions in Longueval and as they did so the Germans maintained sniper fire

---

1   Royal Ulster Rifles Museum, Bedford Street, Belfast. War Diary, 1st Bn RUR June 1944.

and began to probe their defences by sending patrols into and around the village. In turn ambush patrols were sent out to try to counter the German activity. As a result of one of these patrols Marty Vance experienced the loss of the first man in his company, his friend Norman WILLIS nick-named 'Pal Willis'.

Marty VANCE:

'A thing that sticks out in my mind first, there was a fellow commonly known as Pal Willis, he was the first casualty we had in our company. He came from Newcastle Street in Belfast, off the Newtownards Road. He was in the line of fire, one of those things, whether it was a sniper or whatever, we were out on a patrol, and he just got hit, unlucky. These things happen. I felt sorry for him and sorry for the family because I came from the Newtownards Road. Life had to go on, if I started to worry about everybody who was shot or killed it would just affect you that much that you wouldn't be able to carry on.'

The incident involving Norman Willis highlighted the level of assistance provided by the F.F.I. or French Resistance operatives in the area at that time. The ambush patrol of which he was a part was led by Lieutenant R. J. Munro of 'D' Company who took his section South along the bank of the River Orne to the nearby village of Colombelles where an ambush was set up directed at preventing further German infiltration into Longueval. Detail of this incident was recounted by Lieutenant Munro in a report relating to a missing man who was also on the patrol, Corporal R. Cully dated 17th November 1944. The report[2] reads as follows:

My platoon was detailed to set an ambush at Colembelles village. During the action Cpl. Cully was badly wounded in the leg and we had to leave him with a French doctor of the F.F.I. who dressed his

---

2   The National Archives, WO 361/585 Royal Ulster Rifles, Missing, North-West Europe.

wound. *The doctor said they would keep him until we returned.*

It was in late June that I managed to get back to Colembelles and have a look round for Cpl. Cully, but no trace could be found either of him or of the F.F.I. doctor, as the people had all been evacuated from that area.

Only last week Rfm. Cochrane, late of 'B' Coy, who was visiting the battalion and who was also taken prisoner, said he saw Cpl. Cully in a German hospital, so it may perhaps be assumed that he is wounded and a prisoner of war.

During the same ambush, Rfm. Willis was killed instantaneously by a burst of machine-gun fire in the chest. This has been confirmed by Lieutenant Malcolm, 'D' Coy, 1 RUR and also by Cpl. Barr, 'D' Coy.'

Corporal Cully had indeed been taken prisoner of war by the Germans. His name appeared on a list compiled by the International Commission of the Red Cross of prisoners held which indicated that he was imprisoned at Stalag 357 in German-occupied Poland. Stalag 357 was liberated on the 16th April 1945.

Lieutenant Munro's report, although short, tells us quite a lot about the situation on the ground east of the Orne. We do not know how Corporal Cully fell into German hands, nor the identity of the F.F.I. doctor who tended to him. We do now know however that Monsieur Henri DAVOISINE who assisted the men of the 1st Battalion at Longueval was in fact a doctor. When it is considered that his house was used to establish the Battalion Headquarters, that it was also used as a temporary morgue for the dead prior to burial and that he was recorded in the 1st Battalion War Diary as being a source of intelligence for the battalion, it can be assumed that he was an F.F.I. operative. As a doctor in the area, he would have had the all-important access to villages in the locale like Colombelles, where Corporal Cully was entrusted into the care of a F.F.I. doctor and indeed it may have been the case that this access extended to conveying Captain Martin and Bill McConnell

on their daring reconnaissance into Caen. On the face of it both men were left in considerable danger; however, the sighting of Cully in a German hospital by Rifleman Cochrane indicates that whatever the circumstances of his falling into German hands, he was treated well by his captors. If one visits Longueval today little evidence remains of the battles of June 1944. The memorial to the 1st (Airborne) Battalion of the Royal Ulster Rifles who liberated the village stands at the corner of a road junction on 'Route Du Parc' in Longueval, the road forming the junction is named, quite tellingly 'Rue Henri Davoisne'. Dr. Davoisne's house, which for a few weeks in June 1944 housed the Battalion Headquarters alongside the fallen of the 1st RUR which stood at the end of the street which now bears his name.

The River Orne and parallel running canal however created a natural dividing line between two very different regimes of German forces. The 2nd Battalion of the Royal Ulster Rifles were to discover this reality.

2nd Battalion RUR, Le Mesnil

After the first taste of action the men of the 2nd Battalion had plenty to think about as they tried to settle for the night in their slit trenches around Le Mesnil and Anisy. After witnessing their 'D' Company colleagues being knocked back out of the wood at Cambes, just over a kilometre away, the rest of the battalion found it difficult to settle.

Stanley BURROWS:

'When I was lying in that trench, I've got to be honest, from those times right up to the 17th of June, I don't think I really knew any real sleep. If I dozed off it might have been just for a few minutes and your head was shaking and jumping up again. You were always alert and a bit worried in case some German came in the middle of the night and jumped

in with you asleep and came with the cold steel that I didn't have any liking for. That tension was always on you. You didn't really sleep. You were lying in your clothes and dozing off. Maybe later in the war some of the fellows began to get hardened and they could sleep for a while, but I never felt that I could. It was tense at night, and you just couldn't. You had this fear of looking up and a German was standing there ready to take you out.

The next day, after 'D' Company had attacked it, we were told it was too strong in opposition for one company to take and it was ordered that a battalion would go in and attack and capture Cambes Woods and Cambes village.'

On the 8th June 1944 the Battalion Commander Lt. Colonel Ian HARRIS considered the options available to him. Cambes had to be taken to clear the way to Caen. With his 'D' Company now severely depleted he realised that he would have to draw on additional resources to support another battalion-strength attack on the village. There remained the problem of having a lack of intelligence on the strength of the German forces holding the village. During the previous attack a German sleeve identification ribbon had been removed from a dead German, and it was embroidered with the 'Hitlerjugend' title as worn by the noncommissioned officers and men of the 12th SS Panzer Division. This information confirmed the intelligence received the previous evening. Armed with this knowledge Lt. Col. Harris could justify drawing on greater support from other elements on the ground nearby within the 3rd Infantry Brigade area. The 2nd Royal Ulster Rifles were now pitted against an opposition which consisted of elements of both the 21st and the 12th SS Panzer Divisions.

Colonel Harris set about devising a new plan for attack due to take place on the afternoon of the following day, 9th June 1944. His plan for the capture of Cambes by way of a battalion attack

was part of a larger plan involving the whole 9th Infantry Brigade attacking across a roughly five-mile-wide front from Bieville in the East, just opposite the 1st Battalion RUR positions across the Orne to Galmanche in the West. If all the objectives in between were achieved the allied advance would be positioned in an arc just outside the city boundaries to the north of Caen. The objective for Colonel Harris and 2nd RUR was outlined clearly and concisely in his orders,[3] '*2 RUR will capture and consolidate Cambes.*'

To assist in achieving this objective Colonel Harris had a number of additional resources to support the Riflemen. Artillery, in the form of fire support from the six-inch guns of the Royal Navy cruiser HMS *Danae* lying offshore along with the support of the Divisional artillery consisting of one Troop of the 101 Anti-Tank Battery and two Troops of 245 Self Propelled Battery which consisted of eight 17-pounder guns. Additional mortar and medium machine gun support was provided by two mortar platoons and two machine gun platoons from 'B' Company of the 2nd Battalion of the Middlesex Regiment under the command of Major Edmund Lancelot PASSY. The Middlesex men were to position themselves on the left flank of the attack to provide cover to that flank and assist in consolidation after the initial attack. Two squadrons of tanks were made available from the East Riding Yeomanry. Their 'C' and 'A' Squadrons would provide support on the right flank of the attack, to hopefully keep them away from the now known 88mm anti-tank gun positions in La Bijude on the left flank. Further support would be provided by the Royal Engineers with two assault demolition teams and two mine clearance teams made available from 253 Field Company, Royal Engineers. Five Armoured Vehicle Royal Engineers or AVREs as they were known were also provided from 79 Assault Squadron, Royal Engineers. These vehicles were based on a Churchill tank chassis but equipped with a 21 inch 'spigot' mortar specifically developed to destroy hardened bunkers or firing positions. They

3 The National Archives, WO 171/1384, War Diary, 2nd Royal Ulster Rifles.

were particularly effective in that role but only at a range of around 80 yards. They were also equipped with two Besa machine guns. Each Avre carried a crew of five men. The appearance of the Avre vehicles in the order of battle is particularly telling in that it was not known prior to the attack whether there were any hardened enemy structures at Cambes for them to neutralise. An effective reconnaissance had still to be carried out.

Colonel Harris carried out a reconnaissance personally, accompanied by Lt. Colonel WILLIAMSON of the East Riding Yeomanry and Lt. Colonel HUSSEY, the commanding officer of 33 Field Artillery protected by the battalion sniper section. This proved problematic owing to the land between Anisy and Cambes being flat and open for 1500 yards with only a slight rise of about 400 yards from Anisy. Colonel Harris briefed his company commanders on his plan at 16.30hrs on 8th June and instructed that they conduct their own reconnaissance, specific to their individually allotted tasks. In the end, after all of the planning and preparation, what lay in wait behind the high wall at Cambes remained an unknown quantity.

Zero Hour for the attack on Cambes was set for 15.00hrs on the 9th June with the Riflemen due to advance from the start line at Anisy at 15.15hrs following an initial bombardment of the village area.

7

D-Day Plus Three: The Return To Cambes

D-Day Plus Three, Anisy, 15.00hrs

The men of the 2nd Battalion had formed up on the start line for the renewed attack across an 800 yard front on the Southern edge of the village of Anisy. Before them was a straight narrow track, the only feature dividing the wide flat fields of corn that lay for 1400 yards between them and Cambes. 'A' Company formed up in open order to the right of the track with 'B' Company on their right again. Behind and in support were 'C' Company behind 'A' and the depleted 'D' Company behind 'B' company. The flanks of the advance were covered by anti-tank artillery and the Sherman tanks of the east Riding Yeomanry were present to provide further support where required. With the men lined up in open order, bayonets fixed and ready to advance behind the naval artillery barrage they could be excused for likening their experiences and thoughts to those of the previous generation of Ulstermen who stood to face their enemy on a French field just 28 years previously at Thiepval on the 1st July 1916. Perhaps it was exactly that spirit and thinking that carried the day. At 15.15hrs the Royal Ulster Rifles stepped across the start line and commenced a steady advance towards the village of Cambes.

Hamilton LAWRENCE:

'The next day, what they had to do then, Colonel Harris, he called up Brigade and said that there was no way they were going to send one company in, the Battalion weren't going to take it. Colonel Harris contacted the Brigade Commander who was on one of the cruisers and said 'No, we have to go and we have to get more support.' Well, you should have seen the support they gave us that day. They had two batteries of artillery, they had a squadron of fighter planes, they had the cruiser, they had a squadron of tanks, it was fantastic what they had and that was only the support. We lined up again and we got across the wood (at Anisy) and into the open, but what we done, and it was scary, what we call a forward advance. When we got into the open the artillery and the warship was to cover the advance. Now the shells were only landing about a hundred yards in front of you, that was a forward advance or a creeping barrage as they called it. The enemy were firing the other way, but anyway we got there, we had one of the tanks with us and we got into the fields, and we were spread out in a big line in the open air. 'D' Company didn't get to advance because they had nobody left, it was 'A' Company and 'C' Company and the tanks and that were there, it was the yeomanry, the Yorkshire Yeomanry. (East Riding Yeomanry). As soon as we got into the open, in the field itself and over a wee hill, then they opened up with a barrage. One of the tank commanders was in El Alemain and he said in El Alemain as soon as that happened everybody goes down, 'This is where we go to ground, and we're stopped.' Well he was amazed, he said they were dropping all round him but the men carried on. He said he had never seen anything like it.

Anyway, we got there but as soon as we got near their positions and near the wall we were never getting in, they (the tanks) couldn't get in. They couldn't shell the wall and there was no protection anywhere to get in, so a tank managed to bash through the wall, but once it bashed

through it got destroyed, it never got through at all. So, we had to go through without them, once we got through, we got into Cambes. We got in there and of course the enemy knew all the positions, so they waited until they got us in there and in the nighttime, for five hours during the night, non-stop mortar bombing.'

Stanley BURROWS:

'We started off away down in low ground where we couldn't be seen but once we formed up, we for about 1500 yards we didn't know it but the Germans could see us all the way through. When we got into that long corn it was up over our waist, but we advanced at a very steady pace, just as if we were on an exercise. We never felt really yet that we were deep into war because this was the first big battle that we were going to get hit with. So, we advanced with calmness and steadiness and kept the line all the way up. Then, all of a sudden, when we got into the middle, about 1100 yards away, the Germans opened up into what we used to call the 'killing ground'. They let you get into the area where they had their mortars and shells all trained on. When we got into the middle of that the mortars opened up, and also machine guns. Some of the Riflemen would say they never seen any machine gun fire. The mortar fire did the most damage and the men were falling like flies all around us. I seen, in my own company, in my company we had three officers, and everyone was hit. The first I saw was Lieutenant COOPER, he was hit, I didn't know then how severely but he had lost his leg, and he wasn't able to carry on. Lieutenant HALL was hit, and he was killed. We didn't know it then, but we knew he was out of action. My own officer was hit in the head, so we have now three officers out of action. We have no platoon officers; my own platoon sergeant was out of action so we had nothing but corporals and lance corporals to take us into action.

My own officer, Lieutenant WALSH, as I said was hit in

the head, and he got up on his knees and I could see him waving his hand for us to advance. Now my own section, we were sitting back a wee bit, there was Lance Corporal WHITE, Corporal O'REILLY and myself as the Bren gunner and five or six other men, there was about nine to eleven of us altogether. When he gave that advance, we got up and we ran forward, when we got to Cambes to the actual wall we had run right through mortar fire and the men were falling all round us. Whether it was a shell of our own or what that had hit the wall but there was a big 'U' shape hole in the wall. We dived through it and this was where 'D' Company had gone in two days before, and immediately we got through that wall the mortar bombs were still falling and there was still some machine gun fire and I advanced and I seen Major Aldworth who was lying there dead with a German officer almost facing head to head about five feet apart, you would have thought they had killed each other, that's the appearance that it gave you. There was Germans lying dead around them and our people lying dead around them. We had left four wounded, and we didn't know this until later but the SS German Panzer Division who we were up against executed each of the four of them with a bullet to the head, Colonel Harris told us that later. When we saw these bodies, we hadn't time to stop or to do anything, in battle you are not allowed to stop to help your comrade because if everybody stopped only half of the men would end up in action, so you are trained to push on. We went right up through that wood, now the wood was very thickly populated with trees, not like it is today, and there were German trenches all round. The eleven of us fought our way up the left-hand side until we got up to a big farmhouse. When we got to the farmhouse, we took up positions there to cover any Germans who might try to break through again. As we went forward the corporal said to me to jump into the trench and give him cover, it was a German trench, and we were wary of jumping into them in case they were

mined. When I jumped into it I saw this hand grenade, we used to call it a potato masher it was one of the German ones with a long stick on it, I was going to lift it and throw it into the house but all of a sudden I spotted a tiny wire on it so I thought it was booby trapped so I left it alone. I brought my Bren gun up to cover the house and just as I was covering it and the rest of the section were moving forward to take the house, all of a sudden up came a tank at the side of us, one of our own. He let a blast out and he took half of the side of the house away, so he solved our problem there. When we got into the house it was full of German uniforms, they had retreated out the back and got away, so I didn't get a chance to get at them.

The Corporal asked for a volunteer to go back and tell the Battalion where we were. I volunteered not because I was any more of a hero than anyone else, but some instinct made me get up and I volunteered to go back. I handed my Bren gun over to Lance Corporal White and I took his rifle and I started to run down through these big thick woods shouting at the top of my voice 'Don't fire, don't fire' because nobody would have mistaken my voice for a German's as it was a good old Ulster voice, and nobody would have mistaken that. I ran right through the mortar fire and right through the wall where I came from and having already advanced over 1500 yards up there, I was now going back there again. I was really out of breath, and I was heart scared of one of our own riflemen shooting me, because they didn't know where we were, mistaking me for a German. When I got down to the 2 I/C (second in command) Captain Bird at the time, I was standing in front of him with my hands on my lap and I hadn't a breath. I couldn't get out of me what I had to say to him, the next minute he said to me, 'Get it out man and stop your spluttering!' Well, I was angry, if ever I felt like shooting an officer it was that day. But glad to say the Lord restrained me and it was only a passing thought because as it turned out he was a very, very brave officer

who later in the war led 'D' Company as a major and was awarded the Military Cross, but in that moment, I was very angry at his comments. After I thought about it, I realised that he wanted information as quick as he could and I couldn't get it out as fast as he wanted it. That's what had got me angry at him, treating me the way he did, but anyway he was a good officer. I led them right up to where we were, and 'A' Company then took cover there and we surrounded the wood.

For five solid hours we were mortared and shelled, no machine guns now just mortars and shells. We lost a tremendous number of men, somewhere near 200 wounded or killed. That is a powerful lot out of a battalion wounded or killed on that particular day. I could hear the squeals of some men who were hit, to this very day I can hear them. I remember one, I think it was Corporal BOYD, his father worked at the *Belfast Telegraph*, and he had been very badly wounded in the legs, I don't know whether he lost them or not but you could hear men like this. In spite of it all they were cheerful and in a very good mood to be wounded so severely but it was a sight not to see. To see some of your own comrades like SCOTT and Corporal CLOSE who were killed in that attack. These were friends who you had been soldiering with all your life and it hit you, it hit you hard and yet you couldn't stop to help one of them. You saw them falling beside you, but you couldn't stop to help them and this was the hard part of it. You knew you had to go on and you knew the battle had to be kept at it and you kept at it and you kept going and it wasn't until afterwards when you stopped and started to defend the woods and you looked back and saw your mates there, some of them wounded so badly and some of them killed that it really hit you and it really came home to you. You were very sad about it but you had to keep it out of your mind, you haven't to let it get to you, and it would have got to you if you let it. You had to just forget about it and get on with the soldiering and get

on with the job that you were trained to do, hard and all as it was.'

Richard KEEGAN:

'On the 9th then we made a second attack across the same corn field. The shelling was heavier on this occasion and the 88's were heavier, they came down like rain. The only bloke that I seen wounded was a wee Corporal SHIELDS, he was sitting, and the thigh was blew out of him and he was looking water and I daren't stop because once you were on the attack you had to keep moving. I just done that (waved) so that the medical fellows would have a rough idea where he was, and I went on. This tank was hit, and I could hear the men squealing in it, they couldn't get out. Whether the fellow who was in the turret had been shot and killed and was stuck there and they couldn't get out then but the squeals of them inside…you couldn't get near it to touch it because it was red hot with the shells going off inside it. Well, I kept going on anyway and the next thing, I would say it wouldn't have been any more than six or eight yards from me, I seen this thing land and explode and the next thing, I had got it. I must have been 200 yards from the wood whenever I seen the thing land, I actually seen it land and blow up. But I didn't go down, I didn't fall or anything like that and I don't know why that whenever I got hit, it was as high as my shoulder, but I didn't get hit on my head or anything, I wonder did I duck my head, but I can't remember. Anyway, I walked on and the first time we went in on that attack I remember that there were big square holes dug in that field, whether they were listening posts or machine gun posts I don't know which but there was nothing in it the day I passed it on the second occasion, I walked on anyway and there was a ditch for a tank to back into but there was no tank in it so I went in there and at that two stretcher bearers came in, they were the buglers in the battalion. They did first aid on me, and I did first aid

on them! They had been walking along and a bullet had went through one knee and through the other fellow's knee behind him! We got back to the Jeep and back to our own medical unit and got treated there and we were put on a Jeep that night and moved back to the beachhead. We were put into a big tent on the beachhead, the tent was full and the orderlies there looked after them well. I just more or less thought that I'd got a 'blighty one' and that was it, that's all you thought about in them days, get a 'blighty one' and be sent home. I had bits of shrapnel in me from my shoulder down.

In my eyes, and I'm not trying to blow that I'm a brave man or anything like that, but any of those men that went in on any of those actions that I took part in, well they were all heroes, all heroes there is no doubt about it. In their attitude and the way, they went about it and all the rest. This is where the discipline comes in, the discipline of the barrack square and then you discipline yourself. You know you have a job to do so you carry on doing it, you can't stop with that man, even he was your best friend, you can't stop with him, you've got to carry on and make that attack.'

The Battalion War Diary[1] in conjunction with the official Regimental History recorded the casualties following the attack as follows: Three officers and forty-one other ranks killed. Seven officers and one hundred and thirty-one other ranks wounded and evacuated, as in the case of Richard Keegan to the beachhead field hospital. Three officers and three other ranks were wounded but remained with the battalion with one further officer and ten other ranks recorded as missing in action. The total depleted from the battalion fighting strength of both wounded, killed or missing amounted to eleven officers and one hundred and eighty-two men. The Regimental History records the wounding of Corporal Boyd whom Stanley Burrows had witnessed during his

---

1   The National Archives, WO 171/1384, War Diary, 2nd Royal Ulster Rifles.

advance. Corporal Boyd was in command of an anti-tank gun and carrier when the gun received a direct hit from a German 88mm gun. Corporal Boyd was hit and severely wounded along with Rifleman HEALD who received shrapnel wounds to his shoulder with Rifleman Stanley BINGHAM killed in the strike. Rifleman WALTON, the remaining member of the gun crew survived unwounded. The gun was later recovered and brought back into action.

Significantly Captain RYAN of the headquarters Company received severe burns to his hands and knee following the explosion of a phosphorous grenade resulting in his evacuation to hospital. It was Ryan who had recorded the deployment of Rifleman Whitehorn to the SS *Sambut* on the handwritten list which was lodged at the Royal Ulster Rifles Museum years later, the now-important document having been retained in his possession throughout the process of his evacuation.

In the formal orders for the attack on Cambes each company was allocated two objectives which were to be taken and consolidated. Once 'A' and 'B' company's two objectives were taken which essentially covered the eastern and western flanks of the village as far as the church, the centre point of the village, 'C' and the under-strength 'D' Company were to leap-frog through the held positions to take and hold their objectives along the southern edge, the main feature being a small railway halt and building described as being about the size of a signal box. The code words, transmitted back to Battalion Headquarters to signify that these positions were taken were named after the commanding officers of each company responsible for taking them; Objectives 'A1' and 'A2' which covered a road and light railway crossing, were codenamed 'Digger One' and 'Digger Two' after the 'A' Company commander Major Tighe-Wood whose nickname within the battalion was 'Digger'. The 'B' Company points were named 'John One' and 'John Two' after their company commander Major John Hyde. The 'C' company objective code words were

'Stewart Three' and 'Stewart Four' relating to their commander Major Stuart De Longueuil with 'D' company allocated the code words 'Jimmy Three' and 'Jimmy Four' corresponding to Captain James Montgomery who had been given temporary command of 'D' Company following the death of Major Aldworth two days previously.

A further appreciation of the battle for Cambes on the 9th June 1944 can be found within the pages of the London Gazette which contain the citations for gallantry awards made in connection with the action that day. Major TIGHE-WOOD was awarded the Military Cross in recognition of his taking of the first objectives, points 'Digger One' and 'Digger Two'. These two areas encompass the area which included the corner of the wall surrounding the village of Cambes with the deadly 'U' shaped hole described by Hamilton Lawrence. Today, this area is where the memorial to the 2nd Battalion of the Royal Ulster Rifles stands at the end of the road from Le Mesnil now appropriately named Chemin des Royal Ulster Rifles. The wording of the citation[2] to his award sets the scene on the approach to the village as described by the witnesses interviewed:

'Major Tighe-Wood was in command of 'A' Coy, 2 RUR on 9 June 1944 when the battalion attacked the Germans at Cambes. The approach to the objective is open country practically devoid of cover. This was covered by enemy machine gun, mortar and artillery fire. Major Tighe-Wood led his company to the objective, in front of which was a terrific barrage of mortar fire. The Coy advanced through this barrage without a moment's hesitation though they suffered heavily and captured the first objective. The enemy continued to bring down intensive fire on this objective, but despite the fact that all his platoon commanders were either killed or wounded Major Tighe-Wood, by his example of coolness and determined leadership succeeded in establishing his company on the second objective and drove the

2 The National Archives, T/Major WD Tighe-Wood, WO 373/48/189

enemy off. Still under heavy fire he conducted the consolidation of the position without any regard for his own safety. By his brave and determined leadership Major Tighe-Wood was largely responsible for the success of the Battalion's attack.'

The highest award made was that earned by Corporal Cornelius O'REILLY of 'A' Company who led Stanley Burrows' platoon to take the objective of the northeast corner of the village as described by Stanley in his interview, the same area as described in the citation for Major Tighe-Woods' Military Cross. Corporal O'Reilly was awarded the Distinguished Conduct Medal, an award second only in class for gallantry to the Victoria Cross, it was presented to him on the 27th July 1944 along with Military Medal awards presented to Riflemen Jeremiah LONG and Hugh McGLENNON also for action at Cambes on the 9th June 1944. The awards were presented by the Commander in Chief, Field Marshal Sir Bernard Montgomery. Corporal O'Reilly's medal citation reads[3]:

'This NCO was in command of a Rifle Section during the attack at Cambes. His Platoon Commander was killed and the Platoon Sergeant wounded. During the fighting considerable confusion arose and this NCO gathered the men around him and led them with outstanding bravery and leadership. On reorganising he took over command of the platoon, leading them during a difficult period of mortaring on the objective with determination and leadership which inspired and kept them steady.'

The citation reads just as Stanley Burrows recalled his attack, led by the corporal.

Rifleman Jeremiah Long's Military Medal citation related to the incident also described by Stanley Burrows as involving Corporal Boyd and the anti-tank gun crew. The incident was witnessed

---

3 The National Archives, Cpl. C O'Reilly, WO 373/48/235

personally by Lt. Col Harris who submitted the recommendation for the award, the citation reads[4]:

'On the 9th June 1944 this man was attached to a company initially in reserve as a signaller during the attack on Cambes. During the advance to the first objective a carrier towing an anti-tank gun was knocked out by an 88mm anti-tank gun and the crew seriously wounded. Despite heavy machine gun and mortar fire Rifleman Long, who was taking cover by a hedge nearby, immediately went to the assistance of the wounded personnel in the carrier. He made them as comfortable as possible and returned for the company stretcher bearers, leading them back to the carrier.

In crossing the open bullet swept ground Rifleman Long showed great bravery and complete disregard for his own personal safety.'

Corporal Eric BOYD of Cregagh in Belfast was treated and had his injuries recorded by Sergeant Drumgoole before he was evacuated to the Field Hospital at Hermanville. He succumbed to his wounds and died the following day. He rests at Hermanville War Cemetery.

The citation for Rifleman McGlennon's Military Medal award[5], aside from exemplifying his bravery, gives us further insight into the situation that prevailed in Cambes after the objectives had been taken as the 'runner' to the commander of 'D' Company he carried the communications between Captain Montgomery and Battalion Headquarters:

'Rifleman McGlennon is Company Commander's runner of 'D' Coy, 2 RUR. On the evening of 9 June 1944 'D' Coy was ordered to take up a defensive position to consolidate ground won on the capture of the village of Cambes. While 'D' Coy was occupying its position and for four hours afterwards the company was submitted to extremely

---

4   The National Archives, Rfm. J Long, WO 373/48/424
5   The National Archives, Rfn H McGlennon, WO 373/48/425

severe mortar and shell fire and all communications with Battalion HQ and other companies were out of action. Throughout this time Rifleman McGlennon kept his company commander in contact with Bn. HQ and showed complete disregard for his own safety whilst carrying messages at frequent intervals under tremendous volume of fire.'

Captain James MONTGOMERY was awarded the Military Cross for his role in leading the understrength 'D' Company back into Cambes for a second time and taking his objectives 'Jimmy Three' and 'Jimmy Four' on the Southern edge of the village beyond the village church; again his medal citation gives us insight into the conditions on the ground at the time[6]. Reading between the lines of the citation one can perceive the sense of determination harboured by him in completing the job which had been begun by his fallen commander, Major Aldworth two days before.

'During an attack by 2 RUR on an enemy position at Cambes on 9th June 1944 Capt. Montgomery was in command of 'D' Company, having only taken over command on 8 June when his Company Commander was killed. On reaching the objective the company position was subjected to very severe mortar and shell fire and both Captain Montgomery and his 2I/C were wounded. Captain Montgomery refused to have his wounds attended to until he saw that his company was securely established on its objective, and he supervised this part of the operation with the utmost gallantry. The houses which 'D' Company held during the consolidation of this objective were reduced to a mass of rubble but nevertheless the position was held, and the maintenance of the position was of paramount importance in the ultimate success of the attack. The effect of Captain Montgomery's gallant determination in ensuring that his company's position was consolidated was a vital factor in the achievement by the battalion of its objective.'

6 The National Archives, T/Capt. J Montgomery, WO 373/48/190

D-Day Plus Three, 'Jimmy Four', Cambes, 16.10hrs

At 16.10hrs on the 9th June 1944 the signal flare, indicating that all objectives in Cambes had been taken, was fired into the air and observed by staff at 9 Infantry Brigade Headquarters established in the nearby village of Cazelle. All radio communications between Brigade Headquarters and 2 RUR had been knocked out of action and as a result the exact situation on the ground could not be established until an additional replacement radio set could be brought forward into the village. In the interim, according to the plan of attack and in the absence of information, the 1st Battalion Kings Own Scottish Borderers were ordered to advance two companies into the captured village and assist the Royal Ulster Rifles in consolidating their hard-won positions. The heavy price in taking Cambes was not borne by the Ulster Riflemen alone. Those units brought into the battle as support suffered almost as many fatalities as the RUR with the Kings Own Scottish Borderers suffering eight men killed in action.

Five 'Armoured Vehicle Royal Engineers' (AVREs) which were Royal Engineer vehicles built to specific configuration onto a Churchill tank chassis were deployed at Cambes in support of the Royal Ulster Rifles. These vehicles, operated by men from the Royal Engineers 79 Assault Squadron were primarily armed with a 29mm Petard Spigot mortar designed to take out hardened bunkers and defensive buildings with a 40 lb high explosive shell at an effective range of about 80 yards. The AVREs quickly found themselves exposed during the 1500-yard advance across the open ground between Anisy and Cambes and were reduced to defending themselves with their two mounted Besa machine guns during the attack. Four out of the five vehicles, each with a crew of five men, were picked off by the German 88mm guns positioned at La Bijude, East of Cambes, victims perhaps of the gap in intelligence prior to the assault as it transpired that there were no hardened strongpoints behind the elusive walls of Cambes.

Despite being technically at a disadvantage, the AVREs gave a good account of themselves. In the Regimental History their efforts were recorded as follows[7]:

"'A' and 'B' Companies reached their first objective by 1630hrs. In passing through 'A' Company, 'C' Company, who by this time had the Armoured Vehicle Royal Engineers tanks under command, lost these to German 88mm guns firing from La Bijude. These tanks manned by Royal Engineers had done great work, their crews having shown a strong desire to get to grips with the enemy carrying out tasks which strictly they were not intended to do. However, 'C' Company Commander J.C.S.G. de Longueuil could not communicate with them during the battle, and they fought until their tanks were knocked out underneath them.'

79 Assault Squadron, Royal Engineers lost 7 men killed in action at Cambes. Lance Sergeant Wolfe ZIMMERMAN, Sapper Fred EASTOE and Sapper Wilfred ARWELL with Lance Sergeant George ARCHER, Lance Sergeant Lot QUENBY and Sappers John William SMITH and Fredrick HIRST were killed but who remain 'missing in action' unfortunately an indication that their bodies could not be recovered from the burnt-out remains of their vehicles.

The German 88mm artillery pieces deployed in the defence of Cambes provided the defending Germans with a weapon system that was both devastating in effect and clinically accurate. Positioned as they were at La Bijude and firing across the left flank of the attack these artillery pieces were well within effective range of the Riflemen's advance from Anisy, particularly as the advancing troops reached the slight rise in ground some 400 yards across the corn field. The various armoured vehicles supporting the attack across the same ground presented a higher profile target for the 88s to range onto. The 8.8cm Flak 36, to give its proper title,

7   The National Archives, WO 171/1384, War Diary, 2nd Royal Ulster Rifles.

was a dual-purpose gun designed initially to engage air targets but was found to be highly effective against armoured vehicles. By 1944 a range of projectiles were available for use with this weapon including a timed fuse projectile which could detonate at a set range with an air-burst effect rendering it deadly to infantry, both in the open, as in the advance to Cambes or even when sheltering in trenches. All of the veterans interviewed made mention of this weapon, a testimony to the level of respect with which they afforded it and its deadly presence on the battlefield.

Also in support, as part of the 9th Infantry Brigade, were the 2nd Battalion The Middlesex Regiment who had positioned two mortar platoons and two medium machine gun platoons from their 'B' Company in the woods at Cazelle on the left flank of the attack. These units joined in with the initial barrage on Cambes with their mortars and guns. As the Royal Ulster Rifles reached the walled perimeter of Cambes, a further platoon of Middlesex Regiment men, led by the Company Commander Major Edmund PASSY, made their way down the road from Anisy in carriers, light armoured reconnaissance vehicles designed to carry the support weapons relied upon by infantry battalions, with the objective of consolidating the RUR positions. These carriers unfortunately became held up behind infantry who had become pinned down just before the village wall. Once stationary they became sitting targets for the German 88s. One carrier was hit with the crew escaping injury but a second received a direct hit from mortar fire. This vehicle was Major Passy's carrier; the Major was killed outright along with his driver, Corporal Edward GREEN, Lance Corporal Colin REES and Private Victor BAKER. The Company Sergeant Major Nicholas BELL, who was accompanying the Major, was mortally wounded and died of his wounds the following day. The Middlesex Regiment 'B' Company Second in Command, Captain Leonard McDOWELL on hearing that Major Passy had been killed made his way into Cambes Wood from Anisy and was killed almost immediately on arrival by mortar fire. He had just

been told that his wife had given birth to a son.

33 Field Regiment of the Royal Artillery provided artillery support at Cambes; an account of the action from their Regimental History reads as follows:

'At 1500hrs 9th June 9 British Infantry Brigade began the attack on Cambes Wood which was to prove so costly to the regiment. 9 Brigade attacked with 2 RUR with whom were 113/114 Field Battery – Major D.M. BROOKE MC RA, Captains L.L. COBLEY and M.E. ROOSE RA. Under command were East Riding Yeomanry with Captain J.R. Hampson RA. The fire plan was in two phases and called for the firing of concentrations on a timed programme. At about 1630hrs Heaadquarters Royal Artillery informed Regimental Headquarters that it was feared that Lt. Colonel T.E. HUSSEY RA and Lieutenant REDMORE RA had become casualties. It was later confirmed that Lt. Col. Hussey had been killed instantly by an 88mm firing over open sights in a forward position. Major Brooke had gone forward on foot but had not kept in touch with his relay station, and anxiety for his safety was confirmed at about 1800hrs, when Battalion HQ, 2 RUR, telephoned that he had been killed by a direct hit from a mortar bomb. Towards dusk Cambes was captured but there was another casualty as Captain M.E. Roose RA was killed by a shell splinter when entering the village in his tank. 113/114 Field Battery suffered further casualties when Captain L.L. Cobley's Observation Post party were all wounded.'

Tank support was provided by the East Riding Yeomanry (ERY) with a squadron of Sherman tanks. Again, these vehicles fell prey to the German 88mm guns as they moved across the open landscape. A total of six men were lost by the ERY, Lieutenant David BROOKE, Corporal John JACK, troopers Richard NORRIS and Ron GILES. Their bodies were never recovered and again, they remain 'missing in action' with their names remembered on the Bayeux Memorial to The Missing. One other tank crewman

was killed in action, Lance Corporal John DUNNE; his body was recovered and buried initially between Anisy and Le Mesnil, possibly an indication of his final position during the battle. His body was later exhumed and re-buried at La Deliverande British Cemetery where he rests today.

John Dunne's friend Corporal Joseph PRIESTLEY was a dispatch rider with the East Riding Yeomanry. He had landed three days earlier at Lyon-sur-Mer on board a modified Duplex Drive or 'DD' tank which had a limited amphibious capability. His motorcycle had been tied to the side of the tank until after the beach landing. Joseph kept a handwritten account of his time serving in Normandy and in it he described the action at Cambes[8]:

'June 9th, Friday D4. Stand to 3.30am, jerry plane over, no one bothers. Tanks go into action Cambes Wood to support RUR, it sounds like all hell let loose. Our tanks are getting knocked out, mortar fire closer. Johnny Dunne has been reported killed. That news knocked the wind out of me I can't believe it. The battle goes on to 12.30 at night. This is Black Friday for me, I feel in the dumps.

June 10th Saturday D5. Johnnies' death has been confirmed. Jerry planes over, we take up our scrap where we left off. RURs have taken Cambes Wood. On recon with the CO as his bodyguard, sniper gave us a rough time, got back OK. Harbour for night in German billets at Cazelle, plenty of mines and booby traps, jerry left in a hurry and did not set them. Had bath in 2 buckets, mortar fire during night.'

In total 6 officers and 25 men were killed from among those units supporting the Royal Ulster Rifles in the attack at Cambes; the total number of additional wounded cannot be established. The casualty figures recorded for the 2nd Royal Ulster Rifles require a certain scrutiny in order to establish an accurate figure.

8   Joseph B Priestley, 'Diary of a soldier of the East Riding Yeomanry' Priestley family collection, courtesy Mr. S Carr, Australia.

Both the Battalion War Diary entry and the Regimental History state the casualty figures for 9th June in a manner as follows[9]:

'At the end of the day the battalion's casualties were three Officers and forty-one Other Ranks killed, seven Officers and a hundred and thirty-one Other Ranks wounded and evacuated, three Officers and three Other Ranks wounded and not evacuated, one Officer and ten Other Ranks missing.'

The phrase at the beginning of this report *'At the end of the day...',* gives the impression that the three officers and forty-one men killed lost their lives on the 9th June 1944. This is not the case, an examination of the records held and made available online by the Commonwealth War Graves Commission indicate that two officers along with twenty-four men were killed on the 9th June. It appears that the figures recorded represent a total loss for the taking of Cambes-en-Plaine over the three days of fighting between the 7th and 9th June 1944 with one officer, Major Aldworth and 16 men killed on the 7th of June. Of those initially recorded as 'missing' all except two eventually made it back to the battalion. [10]Lance Corporal J. McGOVERN who was initially reported as missing on the 7th June 1944 and Rifleman J. HASLETT who was recorded as missing the following day were both later listed as being held at Stalag IV B Prisoner of War camp at Muhlberg in Germany.

On the 14th October 1980 Hubert Meyer recorded a testimony as part of his research for his publication, *The 12th SS, Volume 1.* He recorded an account from ex Schütze (private) Emil WERNER. Werner had been part of No. 3 Kompanie of the 1st Battalion, 25th SS Panzergrenadier Regiment and was involved in the fighting

---

9   The National Archives, WO 171/1384, War Diary, 2nd Royal Ulster Rifles.
10 The National Archives, WO 361/585 Royal Ulster Rifles, Missing, North-West Europe.

at Cambes of 7th June 1944. As part of his recollections[11], he recorded the following:

'The order came 'Let's go! March!' Everything went well until Cambes. We could see the village very well from our location. At the edge of town, we received infantry fire. All hell broke loose. We stormed a church in which sharpshooters were entrenched. Here I saw the first dead comrade from our company. He was SS grenadier (private) Rühl. I turned him over myself, he had taken a bullet in the head. We had not seen any Englishmen yet, but already we had dead comrades. Then the situation was becoming very critical. My group commander was wounded in the arm and had to go back. SS Grenadier Grosse from Hamburg jumped up past me towards some bushes, his machine pistol at the ready. He shouted 'Hands up! Hands up!' and was successful. Two English soldiers came out with their hands up. As far as I know Grosse was awarded the Iron Cross II for this feat.'

An Oral History account exists in the form of an audio recording mad by a Non-Commissioned Officer, Robert COUPLAND of the East Riding Yeomanry who was in charge of a Sherman 'Firefly' tank in action at Cambes that day, part of two squadrons supporting 'D' Company of the Royal Ulster Rifles on the 7th June. Robert was interviewed on the 19th January 1998 and with regard to the attack he recalled the following[12]:

Robert COUPLAND:
'The Germans, they had made platforms up in trees so they could see anything at a distance... We moved into a position off what was Cambes Junction, it was a small

---

11 Hubert Meyer, 'The 12th SS Vol. One – The History of the Hitler Youth Panzer Division' J.J. Fedorowicz Publishing Inc. 1994, Stockpole Books editions 2005, 2021.

12 I.W.M. Audio Recording, Interview with Robert Coupland, Catalogue No. 17746.

halt on the railway line. Over to our left towards a place called La Bijude there was a Churchill out of the AVRE's, the Armoured Vehicle Royal Engineers; in place of a gun there it had a spigot mortar which would chuck a mortar bomb the size of a five-gallon oil drum, which had some power in it. It had been knocked out unfortunately but this Mark IV, the 'Jerry' (German) tank was stood there, and I just told my gunner to bead on that. The first shot we fired with the seventeen-pounder armoured piercing, woof, he was out, that Mark IV was gone. By the end of shall we say the mid afternoon I had lost two tanks. One with the complete crew, we didn't know what had happened to them till afterwards. The other one was a corporal's tank. He got hit and the co-driver got injured and I said out the lot of you, get out of there and they got on the back of my tank, there was a platform there, the engine cover… I took these lads away, the four of them, the fifth one, the driver, I didn't know what had happened to him at the time. When I went back to where one of the other troop's tanks was, an officer George JENKIN was there and I saw the driver, I didn't know what had happened to him, he was being marched away by a 'Jerry' in a black uniform, that meant the Gestapo (SS). He had a Royal Ulster Rifle boy with him as they were the support infantry. I daren't do anything, I daren't fire at them as we could have killed one of those two and not the German. You know we never heard a thing about that lad, nothing. We wrote to the Commonwealth War Graves Commission for a full list of all the graves and the boys buried in them and there has never been a word of him and I'm very frightened that they disposed of him, killed him, I'm sure of it. (His name was) Walker, Hash Walker. This was the 7th of June and then we withdrew to our harbouring area, which was a chateau, Cazelle Chateau.'

Trooper Fred WALKER was reported as missing in action on the 7th June 1944 at Cambes. His body was never recovered. He is

remembered on the Bayeux Memorial to The Missing. Four weeks later, on the 8th July 1944, Robert Coupland was blinded by a mortar shell explosion.

We can say that the account of Emil Werner recounted by Hubert Meyer describes the capture of Lance Corporal McGovern and Rifleman Haslett. Robert Coupland may have seen one or other of the men after their initial capture. These accounts are significant as both men survived the action in Cambes but more importantly survived being taken prisoner of war. Their capture in this manner, and the subsequent award made to Grenadier Grosse, as we will see, was very much the exception rather than the rule with regards to the actions of the 12th SS Panzer Division. The fate of Trooper Walker remains unknown and may be evidence of another more sinister outcome.

To return to Stanley BURROWS and his description of the attack at Cambes on the 9th June 1944, he made the following comment: *'We had left four wounded, and we didn't know this until later but the SS German Panzer Division who we were up against executed each of the four of them with a bullet to the head, Colonel Harris told us that later.'*

On the face of it, Stanley's comment, although technically hearsay and volunteered almost sixty years after the event, indicated that an additional category should be added when recording those lost at Cambes-en-Plaine on the 7th June 1944. In addition to killed, wounded, and missing, the word 'murdered' should be added.

8

Hitlerjugend

10th December 1945
Aurich, Germany

On the 10th December 1945 Brigadeführer Kurt MEYER appeared before the first ever Canadian Military War Crimes Court to have been convened. The Court was set up at Aurich in Germany and was presided over by Major-General C. VOKES, CB, CBE, DSO, General Officer Commanding 3 Canadian Infantry Division, Canadian Army Occupation Force. Prosecuting was Lieutenant-Colonel B.J.S. MacDONALD OBE ED, the Commanding Officer of No 1 Canadian War Crimes Investigation Unit. Defending Kurt Meyer was Lieutenant-Colonel M.W. ANDREW DSO – Officer Commanding the Perth Regiment. At 10.00hrs, after the Court was formally opened Brigadeführer Kurt Meyer was arraigned in the following terms[1]:

'The accused, Brigadeführer Kurt Meyer, an officer in the former Waffen SS, then a part of the Armed Forces of the German Reich, now in the charge of 4 Battalion, Royal Winnipeg Rifles, Canadian Army Occupation Force, Canadian Army Overseas, is charged with:

First Charge: Committing a War Crime, in that he, in the Kingdom

---

1 P Whitney Lackenbauer & Chris MV Madsen, 'Kurt Meyer on Trial, a Documentary Record' Canadian Defence Academy Press, 2007.

of Belgium and Republic of France during the year 1943 and prior to the 7th day of June 1944, when Commander of 25 SS Panzer Grenadier Regiment, in violation of the laws and usages of war, incited and counselled troops under his command to deny quarter to Allied troops.

Second Charge: Committing a War Crime, in that he, in the province of Normandy and Republic of France on or about the 7th day of June 1944, as Commander of the 25 SS Panzer Grenadier Regiment, was responsible for the killing of prisoners of war, in violation of the laws and usages of war, when troops under his command killed twenty-three Canadian prisoners of war at or near the Villages of Buron and Authie.

Third Charge: Committing a War Crime, in that he, at his HQ at L'Ancienne Abbaye Ardenne in the Province of Normandy and Republic of France on or about the 8th day of June 1944, when Commander of the 25 SS Panzer Grenadier Regiment, in violation of the laws and usages of war gave orders to troops under his command to kill seven Canadian prisoners of war, and as a result of such orders the said prisoners of war were thereupon shot and killed.

Fourth Charge: (Alternative to the Third Charge) Committing a War Crime, in that he, in the province of Normandy and Republic of France on or about the 8th day of June 1944, as Commander of the 25 SS Panzer Grenadier Regiment, was responsible for the killing of prisoners of war in violation of the laws and usages of war, when troops under his command shot and killed seven Canadian prisoners of war at his HQ at L'Ancienne Abbaye Ardenne.

Fifth Charge: Committing a War Crime, in that he, in the province of Normandy and Republic of France on or about the 7th day of June 1944, as Commander of the 25 SS Panzer Grenadier Regiment, was responsible for the killing of prisoners of war, in violation of the laws

*and usages of war, when troops under his command killed eleven
Canadian prisoners of war other than those referred to in the Third
and Fourth Charges) at his HQ at L'Ancienne Abbaye Ardenne.'*

Kurt Meyer replied 'Not guilty' in answer to each of the charges
put to him. The trial ran for the next eighteen days during which
time Meyer gave evidence accounting for his actions in response
to the allegations placed against him and evidence from a number
of prosecution witnesses. During the trial the public heard for
the first time of the make-up and history of the 12th SS Panzer
Division, Hitlerjugend as it was described to the Court. The Court
also heard Meyer explain under oath the movements and make-
up of the various units under his command during the first days
of the invasion. The information put to Meyer originated from
a number of sworn testimonies made by witnesses along with
evidence recovered from scenes of atrocities which came to light
between the 7th and 21st June 1944. This evidence was gathered
under the authority of a Court of Enquiry set up by the Supreme
Headquarters Allied Expeditionary Force (SHAEF) and led by
their Special Inquiries Section, G-1 Division when it was found
that the conduct of the 12th SS Panzer Division consistently
showed a pattern of brutality and ruthlessness wherever they
appeared across the battlefield. As the allied advance took hold and
the 12th SS were pushed back evidence of this brutality was left in
their wake. The evidence was compiled by the Canadian Army as
it appeared that the war crimes offences were almost exclusively
carried out against Canadian soldiers who became prisoners of
war. Canadian Lieutenant-Colonel B.J.S. MacDONALD OBE
ED led these preliminary enquiries and compiled the report of
evidence against the Hitlerjugend; he later led the prosecution
case against Meyer at Aurich.

To understand the atrocities and what ultimately may have
taken place at Cambes between the 7th and 9th of June 1944, we
have to first understand the make-up and ethos of the Hitlerjugend

Division, the soldiers, their non-commissioned officers and their officers. The word Hitlerjugend translates into English as Hitler Youth. This can be misleading and indeed gave an impression at the time that the battalion was made up of children. The term conjures up images of young teenage boys portrayed in movies and in history footage typically attempting to stall the allied advance during the final Battle for Berlin; in reality these boys were part of the Volksstrum or German Homeguard, a militia unit formed in the final stages of the war. In reality the soldiers of the Hitlerjugend were similar in age to some of those whose interviews we have read who served with the Royal Ulster Rifles, especially when we consider that men like Bill McConnell lied about his age in order to enlist, the difference being that that was an exception; with the Hitlerjugend their age of enlistment was clearly defined and that for a young German man choosing whether to enlist or not was not an option. With the rise of the Nazi Party in Germany from 1933, existing youth organisations were effectively dismantled by the Nazi regime in order to indoctrinate the young with Nazi ideology, part of a wider process of Nazifying the whole of German society. In March 1939 a law required that all children between the age of 10 and 18 years were to join the Hitler Youth organisation; other organisations that would traditionally attract youth interest and attendance like scouting and church groups were suppressed. In the Hitler Youth boys were instructed in military drill, taught how to handle weapons, and participate in individual competitive sports. Girls, as part of the Bund Deutscher Mädel, League of German Girls or BDM as it was known, were instructed in nursing, cooking and how to care for a household and family. By the outbreak of war in 1939 the Nazi regime had effectively established a generation of German youth ready to fight in and support Hitler's war effort.

In early 1943 the then leader of the Hitler Youth Artur AXMANN forwarded a proposal to Reichsführer SS Heinrich HIMMLER that a military division be formed, made up entirely

of Hitler Youth boys. The plan was approved by Adolf HITLER and a division of the Waffen SS was assembled to be known as the 12th SS Panzer Division, Hitlerjugend (HJ). Training began at Beverloo and later at Diest in Belgium for former Hitler Youth members who were born in 1926, thus by 1943 they had attained 17 or 18 years of age. Efforts were made initially to enlist the most promising and enthusiastic members of the Hitler Youth into the Division; later recruits were drafted into it regardless of their wishes. The officers and non-commissioned officers were selected from the most battle-hardened units of the Waffen SS, most being transferred from the infamous 1st SS Panzer Division Leibstandarte SS Adolf Hitler (LSSAH), Hitler's Guard regiment, which has been involved in the most brutal combat on the Russian front. The indoctrination and training of the young HJ recruits at the hands of these senior officers was brutal. The original Corps Commander was Gruppenfuhrer (Lieutenant general) Joseph 'Sepp' DIETRICH and the original Divisional Commander was Fritz WITT. As in other Waffen SS divisions promotions, appointments, discipline and general administration of the Division were dealt with internally via their own SS command structure. Operationally they conformed to tactical decisions and formal orders from superior formation commanders whether they were SS or Heer (Regular Army). As with other Waffen SS units they wore distinctive insignia and uniform which fuelled their elitist attitude; they saw themselves as better soldiers, superior to their Heer counterparts and reinforced that feeling always.

As the allied advance progressed in the weeks following the D-Day landings the 12th SS Division held a defensive line north and northwest of Caen that was gradually pushed back. Following the battle at Carpiquet airfield and the fall of Caen the Division was forced to flee to the east in order to prevent encirclement at the Caen–Falaise pocket. On the 7th September 1944 Kurt Meyer was captured at the Belgium town of Durnal near Namur. He had been making his way east with remnants of his, by this

stage decimated, Division when he came upon a spearhead unit of American troops. He attempted to avoid them and hide in a farm building but was found by the owner. He fled and was spotted by a neighbour who raised the alarm and was eventually surrounded in a shed by Belgian partisans where he gave himself up. Meyer was held initially at a hospital in Namur before being transferred to a prisoner of war camp at Compiegne. On the 26th March 1945 Meyer was interviewed by a preliminary Court of Inquiry held at the London District prisoner of war cage at 7 Kensington Palace Gardens in London. Meyer answered the questions put to him which at that time and a record of his interviews from that point was retained along with evidence of the various atrocities that were believed to be connected with the 12th SS which formed the content of a preliminary report ahead of a formal trial. These initial enquiries were concluded by Colonel MacDonald on the 28th October 1945 and the prosecution case against Meyer was prepared. In total, over a series of incidents which took place after the initial battles of the invasion of Normandy it was believed that no less than 156 captured Canadian soldiers were murdered in the hands of the 12th SS Hitlerjugend. As a statistic, 1 in 6 Canadians killed in Normandy died after capture.

The trial of Kurt Meyer and inquiry leading to it was convened and investigated by the Canadian Military authorities; the victims, with the exception of three, were Canadian soldiers. Meyer's interviews however can shed light on what happened behind the wall at the village of Cambes following the initial attack by 'D' Company of the Royal Ulster Rifles on the evening of the 7th June 1944[2]. On that date, by his own admission, Kurt Meyer held the position of the officer commanding the 25th Panzergrenadier Regiment, part of the 12th Hitlerjugend Division which consisted

---

2   The National Archives, TS 26/856, 'Supplementary Report of the Supreme Headquarters Expeditionary Force Court of Enquiry re Shooting of Allied Prisoners of War by 12 SS Panzer Division (Hitler Jugend) in Normandy, France 7-21 June 1944.'

of three battalions, each with their own commanders. He stated that he was in command of this regiment until a date between the 10th and 15th of June 1944 whereupon he was appointed Divisional Commander of the entire 12th SS Division; this was on account of the death in action of the previous Commander Fritz WITT. Meyer was pushed during interview to provide an exact date of when he took command of the Division but he continually evaded providing a satisfactory answer, only going as far as to say that it was on the day Fritz Witt was killed but not conceding or stating what date that day was. It must be remembered that Meyer was aware that he was being questioned on a number of war crimes carried out across a range of dates and that the principle of vicarious liability was being applied by the inquiry, by answering questions on his level of command responsibility he may have been attempting to deflect that responsibility for dates when he was aware that atrocities were committed passing blame to the deceased Witt. During the interview it was important for Lieutenant Colonel MacDonald to establish exactly which officer oversaw each unit within the Division. In relation to the 7th June 1944 that line of questioning proceeded as follows[3]:

Q. *And who on the 7th June commanded the First Battalion of the 25th Regiment?*
A. *WALDMULLER.*
Q. *And was his rank Sturmbannfuhrer?*
A. *Yes.*
Q. *How long did he continue to command that battalion?*
A. *He was still commanding when I was taken prisoner. I may be mistaken there but I believe so.*
Q. *Who commanded the Second Battalion on the 7th June?*
A. *SCAPPINI.*
Q. *Was he an Italian?*
A. *I think his father came from Italy.*

---

3 Ibid.

Q. What was Scappini's first name?

A. Hanz.

Q. And what was Waldmuller's first name?

A. It was also Hanz, I am sure of this, and I think the name is also right with regard to Scappini.

Q. And how long did Scappini continue to command the Second Battalion?

A. He was killed two days later.

The Inquiry also questioned Meyer with regard to the positions of his 25th Panzergrenadier Battalions from the 7th June 1944. He was shown a map of the area, the 1:50000 Caen 7F/1 War Office series publication. On this map he marked the positions of the three battalions in red along with other information relating to his route of advance from Caen on the 6th/7th June and his various headquarters' positions. Significantly he marked the 1st Battalion position on the 7th June at Épron with a line of intended advance indicated in the direction of Cambes; Épron being approximately two kilometres southeast of Cambes.

Meyer was again questioned about the positioning of his units and his whereabouts on the 7th June 1944 during his actual trial. On this occasion, and under oath, he was more specific with relation to his movements around the 25th Regiment areas but it must be remembered that by this time further atrocities had come to light, notably the murder of a further 18 Canadian prisoners of war at Meyer's Regimental Headquarters at Abbaye d'Ardenne, southwest of Cambes. During this section of questioning Meyer describes seeing wounded Canadians at the Abbaye and then outlines his action afterwards[4]:

A. (Continuing) The total number of wounded I estimated at 50 soldiers. The doctor told me that he had difficulties in evacuating the wounded. The low-flying aircraft who held the area shot

---

4   Ibid.

at every vehicle they could see. I thereupon gave the order to evacuate the wounded during the night, at the beginning of darkness, and then went to the 2nd Battalion.

Q. *What time would this be about, that you went to the 2nd Battalion?*

A. *It must have been about 1800 or 1900 hours. The Battalion was still engaged in fighting and the Battalion Commander was killed just the minute I arrived there.*

Q. *Before you left the Abbaye, did you give any orders other than what you have said to us concerning the prisoners?*

A. *No.*

Q. *On the 7th of June, did you know that there were any Canadian prisoners shot at the Abbaye?*

A. *No.*

Q. *Did you ever give any orders on the 7th of June for Canadian prisoners to be shot?*

A. *No.*

Q. *Go on. You had reached the Battalion Commander of the 2nd Battalion. Go on from there.*

A. *The Commander of the 2nd Battalion was killed by a direct hit from a tank and lost his head. I ordered a new Battalion Commander and put him in the picture.*

Q. *Who was this new Battalion Commander?*

A. *Haupsturmführer Schrott. During this time heavy artillery fire was directed on the area – the Battalion sector. An infantry battle was going on heavily and there was tank and artillery fire.*

Q. *Where was this going on? Where was the 2nd Battalion then?*

A. *North of Contest in the direction of Galmanche. From there I went to the 1st Battalion. This Battalion was engaged in attacking Cambes. That Battalion had withdrawn from the last mentioned village since an enemy tank attack had come in on the left flank, and because the 21st Panzer Division, presumably on account of an error, had not accompanied my attack. I spoke with the*

Battalion Commander and gave the order to defend and keep the conquered positions, and to take up contact in the right to the 21st Panzer Division and to the left with the 2nd Battalion. From the 1st Battalion I drove back to the 2nd Battalion and there I gave the same order changing over from attack to defence and to seek contact with the 1st Battalion. From the 2nd Battalion, I drove to the 3rd Battalion by the garden fields west of Contest, and I wanted to speak to the Battalion Commander.

So from across both sessions of questioning we can establish from Meyer's statements that the Commander of the 1st Battalion 25th Panzergrenadier was Sturmbannführer Hanz WALDMULLER. Further to that we can say that the 1st Battalion were engaged in action in Cambes on the 7th June 1944 and that Meyer met and spoke to Waldmuller in the village that evening and issued him with specific orders to remain there in defensive positions. He later stated to the enquiry that when he returned to his headquarters at Abbaye d'Ardenne after visiting the 2nd and 3rd Battalion commanders it was around 2300hrs. It may well be the case that by describing these inspections Meyer felt perhaps that he was establishing an alibi to take him away from the Abbaye for most of that evening. If this was the case, he must have felt safe in placing himself with Waldmuller at Cambes. Regardless of Meyer's intentions, from his evidence we now know that Sturmbannführer Johann 'Hanz' Waldmuller was the commander of the SS troops whom the men of 'D' Company of the Royal Ulster Rifles encountered behind the wall at Cambes-en-Plaine on the 7th June 1944. Waldmuller had a more direct and heightened level of vicarious liability for the behaviour of his men at that time; he was ultimately responsible for their conduct and in particular in their treatment of prisoners of war.

To reinforce this point, we have to consider the frame of mind of the men of the 25th Panzergrenadiers. Fortunately, compelling evidence was presented to the War Crimes Tribunal at Aurich on

that exact point, which was crucial in convicting Kurt Meyer; the same evidence is equally compelling when read in conjunction with Waldmuller and events at Cambes.

On the 6th January 1945 the Court of Inquiry resumed to hear and record the evidence of a witness, a German soldier who had been taken prisoner of war and who was examined on oath. The witness was introduced to the Court as Grenadier Friedrich TORBANISCH, Prisoner of War, late of 15 Company, 25 Panzer Grenadier Regiment, 12 SS Panzer Division (Hitlerjugend). The verbal evidence he gave was recorded, marked for the Court as 'Exhibit No. 5,' and took the form of a written record of his sworn interview. Grenadier Torbanisch was interviewed by Lieutenant Colonel BORASTON along with Lieutenant Colonel MacDonald; the relevant sections from the transcript are as follows:

Q. *What is your rank?*
A. *Private. Grenadier.*
Q. *To what regiment did you belong when you were taken prisoner? I want to know your unit.*
A. *I was not in the front; I was a deserter since the 4th April. (1944.)*
Q. *From what unit did you desert?*
A. *Fifteenth Company, 25th Regiment, SS Hitlerjugend.*
Q. *What is your age?*
A. *Eighteen- and one-half years. I am going to be nineteen on the 27th March.*
Q. *Where did you live?*
A. *Sassahnfart, near Banberg, Bavaria.*
Q. *What languages do you speak.*
A. *I speak Flemish. I was with the Belgian Resistance movement and worked with them.*
Q. *Do you speak French or English?*
A. *No.*
Q. *When did you first become attached to the 25th SS Panzer Regiment?*

A. 15th June 1943, but it was not voluntary; I was transferred into it.

Q. Had you been in the Hitler Youth organisation prior to that time?

A. We had to belong after our tenth birthday.

Q. Where did you serve with the 25th Regiment?

A. At first, we were in Belgium. Beverloo in Belgium. I was there for training. The railroad station is Bourg Leopold.

Q. Were you given any orders as to what you should do in the event of capturing Allied soldiers?

A. Yes, we were given secret orders.

Q. What were these orders?

A. I gave these to the White Army Intelligence Service.

The 'White Army' referred to by Torbanisch was the Belgian resistance movement known as the 'Witte Brigade'. Amongst carrying out partisan activities the Witte Brigade acted as a scouting and intelligence network in particular providing assistance to the advancing Canadian forces from September 1944.

Q. Did you give these orders from memory, or did you have a copy of them?

A. No, I gave them from memory all that I could remember, but my memory was still very fresh.

Q. How were these orders communicated to you?

A. They were read to us, and we had to sign

Q. What did you sign?

A. That these secret orders were known to us.

Q. When were these orders read to you?

A. That was in April 1944.

Q. And was this while you were in Diest?

A. Yes, in Montague.

Q. Who read the orders to you?

A. The Stabscharführer Spiess. (Equivalent to British Army Company Sergeant Major rank)

Q. What was his name?

A. HAGETORN.

Torbanisch was then shown a copy of the Secret Orders obtained by the enquiry and the following was put to him:

Q. *I show you what purports to be a photographic copy of the orders which you said were read to you; will you look at these papers and see whether they contain the substance of what you remember of the orders that were read to you in April by this Spiess?*

A. *Yes, this paragraph referring to the first one is right. Second paragraph also is correct. The third order is right too. Fourth is correct. That they shouldn't take any prisoners. The second paragraph of the fourth order is right too. The fifth order is right. Sixth order is right. The general paragraph is also right.*

Lt. Col. MacDonald: *These will be entered as Exhibit A1 for the first page and A2 for the second.*

The document that was read to and confirmed as correct by Torbanisch had been dated July 1944, and had been made available to the Court by the Witte Brigade and then Canadian Military Intelligence services as an intelligence report and had essentially then at that point been proven as an evidential Court exhibit. It was subsequently translated into French, Belgian and English to assist the Court, the English copy was marked Exhibit A3[5].

Exhibit A3 Reads as follows:

SECRET
Translation of Flemish part of CX 12401/IV/7260 (Opifex)
Inf: Dated July 44.

25th Regiment SS- Hitlerjugend-Adolf Hitler
SS Troops – 15th Company – Reconnaissance Bn.
Secret Orders

5 Ibid.

1st Order: Attitude towards civilian population in occupied countries. If the population looks contemptuously at an SS soldier or spits at him the person concerned may be beaten and arrested. If the cross-examination results in the impression that the arrested is an Anti-German he shall be secretly executed. ('Terechtgesteld')

2nd Order: If a person tries to get information about weapons and ammunition he shall be arrested and cross-examined in the most rigorous manner. If the cross-examination results in the impression that the arrested is an Anti-German he shall be executed for espionage. The same punishment shall be meted out to soldiers who pass on information about their weapons.

3rd Order: Guards are not allowed to leave their posts, nor are they allowed to eat, drink, sleep, smoke, lay down, let their weapons out of their hands as long as they are on guard duty. Leaving the post before being relieved or passing on of the password to the population shall be punishable by death. The password is the most important thing of guard duties.

4th Order: Attitude at the front: The SS troops shall take no prisoners. Prisoners are to be executed after having been interrogated. The SS soldiers shall not give themselves up and must commit suicide if there is no other choice left. The officers have stated that the British do not take prisoners as far as SS soldiers are concerned.

5th Order: Information about enemy's troop movements are to be communicated quickly. Communications on paper shall, at the same time be learnt by heart. If a soldier gets into danger all papers must be burnt or eaten up. He is to carry nothing but his identity disk. Silence must be kept about everything. The traitors will be executed, even after the war.

6th Order: The observers returning with information from the front

*and accompanying officers shall not take the same route as to the
front.*

The existence of the Secret Orders was shocking. Friedrich
Torbanisch was examined in full by the two investigating Colonels
who established that the giving of the orders was carried out
during an evening parade of the company when all of the men were
instructed to gather closely around the Stabscharfuhrer Hagetorn,
whereupon the instructions were spoken in a low tone to avoid
any eavesdropping. Torbanisch was also questioned regarding his
treatment while in custody and he assured the inquiry that he had
been treated well. The evidence provided by him was not deemed
to have been gained under duress. Although Torbanisch deserted
from the 25th Panzergrenadier Regiment in May 1944, just before
the invasion, his testimony gives us an insight into the mentality of
the enemy whom the Royal Ulster Riflemen faced behind the wall
at Cambes. In stark contrast to what we know of their own training
and background, here was an 18 year old boy, indoctrinated with
Nazi ideology from the age of 10 years, armed, and in effect given
the power to kill members of an occupied civilian population if
they literally so much as looked at him sideways.

The existence of the 'Secret Orders' and the content of the
document was put to Meyer during his trial. He of course denied
any knowledge of such orders. Meyer, during questioning prior to
the production of the incriminating 'Exhibit A' on matters relating
to general command structure, admitted knowing Stabscharfuhrer
Hagetorn and in fact recalled that he was the NCO in charge of the
15th Company based at Montague exactly as Torbanisch had stated.
This was all before the incriminating evidence was produced.
During the course of the preliminary inquiry and eventual trial
an additional three witnesses gave evidence corroborating the
testimony given by the witness Torbanisch.

Further information regarding the activities of the 25th SS
Panzergrenadier Regiment can be obtained from an officer who

later, for a short period, commanded the 12th SS Division after Kurt Meyer's capture. This was Hubert MEYER, not related to Kurt. He survived the war and in 1992 published 'A History of the 12th SS' in two volumes. Hubert Meyer gives a generally triumphalist account of the actions in which the 12th SS were involved. It must be remembered that this work was published in 1992, by which time most war crimes investigations had run their course but could of course still be instigated. It is obvious on reading his work that he was careful with regards to what to include and what to perhaps leave out. Hubert Meyer confirmed the presence of the 25th Panzergrenadier 1st Battalion in Cambes on the 7th June 1944 and specifically mentioned that they engaged the 'Royal Ulsters'.[6] He stated that Kurt Meyer visited the positions at Cambes and met with Hanz Waldmuller. He described an incident during the night after the main battle where British troops recovered a Sherman tank which was abandoned in the centre of Cambes. This incident may relate to the action of Lieutenant George JENKIN of the East Riding Yeomanry. Lt. Jenkin's troop attacked in support of 'D' Company of the Royal Ulster Rifles on their left flank. He could not find a way into the village and was forced to drive the full length of the wall on the East of Cambes before turning down a lane at the railway halt that led to the centre of the village. In doing so he had advanced ahead of the infantry and found himself in the rear of the German positions, taking them by surprise. He was awarded the Military Cross for his actions, his citation best describes what happened:

'On 7 June 1944, Lt. Jenkin's troop was supporting the attack on Cambes when three German tanks engaged them. Knocking out one enemy tank and driving off the remainder, Lt. Jenkin proceeded ahead of the infantry under withering fire into the town. There he

6   Hubert Meyer, 'The 12th SS Vol. One – The History of the Hitler Youth Panzer Division' J.J. Fedorowicz Publishing Inc. 1994, Stockpole Books editions 2005, 2021.

destroyed five enemy vehicles and killed a large number of their infantry. Shortly afterwards Lt. Jenkin was forced to leave his tank to contact the RUR. He found himself unable to return to it owing to enemy fire. Observing two enemy tanks some 1300 yards away, he personally laid a 6 pdr anti-tank gun on to the leader and set it afire. Throughout this operation the coolness and courage of this officer were an inspiration.'

The recovery of Lieutenant Jenkin's tank may have been what was described by Meyer.

Hubert Meyer had referred to war diaries in compiling his history in much the same way as I have done. At this juncture however, in describing the aftermath of the Cambes attack he stated[7]: *'No figures are available of enemy losses in the attack sector of 1 Battalion (25th Panzergrenadiers) they were obviously significant.'* The war diaries and the relevant casualty figures do exist and have been available for many years; it is perhaps the case that he chose to avoid touching on this aspect of what took place at Cambes, they were certainly significant but perhaps for other reasons. At that time, and up to the present day, no prosecutions have been brought about for war crimes violations which took place there. He also omitted to describe the considerable action which took place at the same location on the 9th June 1944. Interestingly he described an incident at Mesnil-Pantry where senior German officers were killed by Canadian 'friendly fire' when they were being brought back to Canadian lines. On describing the incident he quite openly stated, in a frank matter of fact manner[8]: *'In retaliation, three Canadian prisoners were ordered shot near the Command Post of the II/26 (2nd battalion of the 26th Panzergrenadier Regiment) on the following day. After the war a so called 'war criminals trial' took place because of this against Obersturmbannführer Siebken, Untersturmführer*

---

7 Ibid.
8 Ibid.

Schnabel and two men from the battalion.' Hubert Meyer was obviously comfortable in stating this as fact because at the time of his writing the two officers named had already been sentenced to death and the sentence carried out, the matter had long been dealt with. The manner in which he dismissed the shooting of the three prisoners as being justified somehow 'In retaliation' and his obvious contempt of the war crimes Court added to the picture already painted of the standard operating procedures of the 12th SS Panzer Division in Normandy during June 1944.

One further case worthy of mention in establishing similar but unconnected facts regarding the apparent brutal standard practice in their treatment of prisoners of war by the Hitlerjugend is the case of British Royal Engineer Sapper Richard Barclay FORBES.[9] On the 12th June 1944 at Les Fains, a village approximately twelve miles southwest of Cambes, Sapper Richard Forbes of Number 2 Troop, 4 Field Squadron of the Royal Engineers was seen by a local French man being escorted by three German soldiers heading south in the direction of Villers Bocage. It is not known how Sapper Forbes fell into enemy hands, however at that time Les Fains was approximately 4 miles beyond the extent of the British lines where a tank battle had taken place around the village of Villy. It was later accepted by an enquiry team that the Sapper could only have been in Le Fains by way of having become a prisoner of war, the village was in German hands. The French witness, a local farmer called Pierre BEAUJAN, had been working in his field at around 16.00hrs as the party passed him. He was concealed by an earth bank and undergrowth about ten metres from the road. Without warning the German soldiers stepped aside and one of them shot the British soldier a number of times at close range with a sub machine gun. The witness

9   The National Archives, WO 219/5051 'Report of the Supreme Headquarters Allied Expeditionary Forces Court of Enquiry re Shooting of an Allied Prisoner of War by the German Armed Forces at Les Fains, Normandy 12 June 1944'

Monsieur Beaujan initially took cover and hid, fearing that he had been seen and then later that evening he made his way to the house of another local farmer Gabriel LELIEVIE, arriving at his farm at around 19.00hrs where he told Mr. Lelievie what he had witnessed. Both men were apprehensive in returning to the scene of the shooting as the German soldiers responsible were actually billeted in the farm outbuildings belonging to Mr Lelievie, so they waited until the next morning and walked along the road to where Mr. Beaujan had witnessed the shooting. There they found the body of the British soldier, partially covered by a blanket, lying in the ditch at the side of the road. His boots had been removed and were missing and the men noted he had gunshot wounds to his head, neck and chest. They also noted that he had a wound on his right arm which had obviously occurred prior to the shooting as it had been dressed with a bandage and the arm was outside of his jacket. There were around eight or nine empty cartridge cases lying on the road close to the body, these cases were still intact and had not been crushed, indicating that no traffic had passed since the shooting took place.

The incident was reported to the local Mayor, Mr. Le Viconte de LUGIS, who made representation to the German authorities to have the body buried. Burial was refused until the 15th June when further representations were made to bury the man for hygienic reasons Mr. Lelievie took part in the burial and he searched the soldier's body before he was interred. All military documents and identity tags had previously been removed from the body, he however found personal letters and photographs wrapped in a waterproof cover, all of which were required to be forwarded on to the Germans via the Mayor and ultimately were held in the chateau belonging to him. Lelievie had the foresight to retain one letter, this he rolled up and placed in a bottle which he sealed with a cork, he then buried the bottle along with the soldier close to where he was shot at the edge of the village thus preserving his identity.

The case of the murder of the sapper was reported to the allied military authorities after the liberation of the village. A Court of Inquiry with investigative powers was held in the local Mairie (town hall) at Le Fains on the 8th October 1944 headed again by Colonels MacDonald and Boraston who conducted the enquiries into the activities of Kurt Meyer. On interviewing Mr. Lelievie a team of investigators went to the site of the burial and exhumed the body, there they found the bottle containing the letter still intact and from it and regimental insignia recovered from the uniform the investigators confirmed that the soldier was Sapper Richard Barclay Forbes, no. 2040362, Royal Engineers. An examination of the body was carried out and it was established that the cause of death was as a result of five gunshot wounds from a small calibre weapon similar to a sub-machine gun, consistent with the report of the witness Beaujan. Unfortunately it was found that Mr. Beaujan had himself been killed some weeks after the incident when the road which he was walking along was strafed by a fighter plane. The enquiry interviewed Mr. Lelievie at length and established that on the 8th June 1944 three German officers and a company of soldiers were billeted in the farm buildings at his property. An officer had told Mr. Lelievie that they belonged to the 30th Panzer Division but he suspected that this was untrue as the German officer discovered that Mr. Lelievie could speak fluent German and became wary of him. In fact, at the time of the shooting no 30th Panzer Division existed but Mr. Lelievie was not to know this. On the evening of the murder when Mr. Beaujan called with him, he actually recognised and pointed out the German soldier who had shot Sapper Forbes, he was one of those billeted at the farm. Mr. Lelievie recognised the man as the same soldier who had threatened to shoot him (Mr. Lelievie) on two occasions over trivial matters while he was stationed at his farm.

Significantly, as part of his evidence, Mr. Lelievie told the court that on the 15th June 1944 he overheard one of the two Obersturmführer (lieutenants) based their issue orders to a group

of ten soldiers in the grounds of the farm. The lieutenant, who was about to carry out a search for an allied pilot who had crashed close by instructed his men that they were not to take prisoners and that 'All prisoners were to be shot'. It can be seen that this German unit, when it came to the taking of prisoners, and for that matter in the treatment of civilians, were complying to a similar set of orders to those that were read to Panzergrenadier Torbanisch two months earlier. Mr. Lelievie then told the court that on arriving at his property the Germans took two of his calves for food. With German efficiency they issued him with a requisition slip with which he could claim back compensation for his loss. He kept this slip as it contained a Waffen SS official stamp and Field Post Office number which he suspected would be unique to the unit and help in identifying the murder of Sapper Forbes. Enquiries were made regarding this number through intelligence sources, and it was discovered that the unit billeted at Le Fains was not the 30th Panzer Division as Lelievie had been told but was in fact the 26th Panzergrenadier Regiment of the 12th SS Hitlerjugend Division which had been fighting alongside their 'sister' 25th Battalion west of Cambes. Descriptions of the German soldier who murdered sapper Forbes and the Obersturmführer who gave the orders to shoot prisoners were distributed among all prisoner of war camps. Instructions were also issued by the inquiry to those in command of prisoner of war facilities to identify and separate any soldiers who had served with the 12th SS Hitlerjugend in order that they be interviewed to establish if they were at Le Fains on the 12th June 1944. No German soldier was ever found responsible for the murder or for issuing the orders. Through the diligence and quick thinking of Mr. Gabriel Lelievie and Mr. Pierre Beaujan Sapper Richard Forbes was afforded the dignity of a marked grave in defiance of those who took his life and left his body in a roadside ditch. On the 10th October 1944 he was finally laid to rest at Hottot-les-Bagues British Cemetery, plot XII, row H, grave 15.

The volume of testimony and evidence contained within

the court papers connected with the trial of Kurt Meyer was considerable to say the least; however, no allegations were ever put to Meyer in relation to the shooting of Royal Ulster Rifles prisoners taken at Cambes on the 7th June 1944. What impact then did the overall ingrained attitudes of the 12th SS Hitlerjugend and the existence of the 'Secret Orders' have on their behaviour there? The initial mention of the matter from the men interviewed in 2003 came from Richard Keegan, he said:

Richard KEEGAN:

'In that wood the Germans were dead crafty, they had personnel bombs and trip wires and all the rest of it tied up in the trees so whether any of the boys had tripped any of them or anything like that I don't know, and that's where they were wounded, but there was some wounded anyway and they were left there... There was a few left behind wounded, you couldn't have dragged them out; the trees were that close together, you would only have done them harm and they were left there for the Germans to look after but the Germans, according to Stanley (Burrows) whenever they went in (on 9th June) they found them all dead, shot.'

Richard's account is reliable, being a member of 'D' Company he was in a position to know what happened behind the wall at Cambes during the initial attack. He was there, the man in the arena. He explains the leaving of the wounded men although he doesn't name them or say how many there were, only that they were left. As to the outcome he relies on what Stanley Burrows has to say. Richard Keegan was wounded and put out of action before he could make it back through the wall again and return to the scene on the 9th of June. Stanley Burrows did fight his way through the wall on the 9th but his consciousness of what took place is based on a subsequent conversation with his commanding officer, Colonel Ian Harris:

Stanley BURROWS:
'We had left four wounded and we didn't know this until later but the SS German Panzer Division who we were up against executed each of the four of them with a bullet to the head, Colonel Harris told us that later.'

Although Stanley had no perception of what had actually taken place the fact that he was told this by his commanding officer adds weight to the idea that it actually did happen. It may have been the case that Colonel Harris told Stanley and the men shortly after the event; in doing so he would have taken a risk on the information having a detrimental effect on morale. It may have been the case that the matter was discussed many years later, perhaps at a Regimental Association reunion, we just don't know. Nothing appears in the official accounts of the action at Cambes within either the War Diary or the Regimental History. A diary however exists written by a Lieutenant of the Royal Ulster Rifles called Cyril RAND, a copy of which is held in the archives of the Royal Ulster Rifles Museum in Belfast; a relevant section is reproduced below with the kind permission of his family.[10]

Lieutenant Cyril RAND:
'As we drew nearer to Cambes 'D' Coy were ordered with a squadron of tanks in support, to attack the village most of which was surrounded by a high stone wall behind which was a narrow belt of trees. As 'D' Company prepared to launch their attack the increased tempo of enemy shelling and machine gun fire became quite noticeable.

With the other Companies who were not taking part we lay in any hollow or shallow depression we were able to scrape out that afforded us some degree of protection. Although a lot of the fire was being directed at the Company

---

10 Cyril Rand, 'From Sword Beach to Troarn' Royal Ulster Rifles Museum, Bedford Street, Belfast. Extract reproduced by kind permission of Mr. P Woodadge.

carrying out the attack we were still being subjected to an uncomfortable amount of shelling.

As I flattened myself as close as possible to the ground, I looked up to see two small birds perched on the branch of a fallen tree, blithely singing and happy completely oblivious of everything that was taking place around them. Amidst all this turmoil, I thought, life still goes on. I just hoped that it would still go on for me too!

To add to our discomfort, we were machine gunned by four German aircraft; the first we had seen: luckily their aim was woefully inaccurate and we suffered no casualties.

Due to the high wall the tanks supporting 'D' Company were unable to provide effective covering fire and the attack was repulsed. As a result Major John Aldworth, the Company Commander and eleven other ranks were killed, and one officer and seventeen other ranks wounded. When some days later, we captured the village, we found John's body, with some of his men, just inside the wood, and a few yards from them were the bodies of several of the enemy who had obviously been engaged in fighting at close quarters. We also discovered a platform built in the trees, from which enemy machine gunners had fired down on the attacking troops. We found too, a grisly example of the callous behaviour of the troops of the 12 SS Division; some of the more severely wounded, unable to walk, had been left in the shelter of a trench outside the village wall when 'D' Company were forced to withdraw. Each of these men were found with a revolver shot through the head.'

Lieutenant Rand's account, corroborated in regard to what we now already know of the battle, even down to the attack from fighter aircraft and observing a platform in the trees, has to be regarded as reliable. He states that there were four men, as did Stanley. In information given to him from Colonel Harris, he also states that each of the four men were wounded to the extent of being unable to walk, again corroborated by Richard Keegan,

but that regardless of and in addition to their pressing wounds, whether they were mortal wounds or not, they each were found, 'with a revolver shot through the head'. These final seven words of his account tell us more, the use of the word 'through' along with the earlier use of the word 'grisly' in his account paint a macabre picture of a cold-blooded close-range, point-blank killing. To put it bluntly, an execution of men unable to defend themselves. A reader on considering Rand's account may pick up on the use of the word 'revolver', which of course describes a specific type of handgun where rounds are chambered using a revolving cylinder and may as devil's advocate, question how Lieutenant Rand could have known a revolver was used when he didn't actually see what weapon was employed. The alternate term would perhaps be the word 'pistol' which would be more in line with the weapon issued to German officers at that time, most likely the distinctive Luger P 08 9mm automatic pistol.

Research with a forensic firearms expert clarified the matter in that the British infantry officer (not being Airborne or SAS) at that time was issued with a .38 Enfield revolver. The 'Instructions for Armourers' book, updated in 1936 relating to this weapon was titled, 'Supplement No.1, Pistols, Revolver No.2 Mark 1 (.38-inch with 5-inch barrel)'. To Cyril Rand therefore, an officer's sidearm could be and was described as either a pistol or a revolver. He used the term most commonly used by him based on the sidearm he carried. From the accounts made I feel that beyond doubt four men of 2nd Battalion The Royal Ulster Rifles, wounded prisoners of war, were murdered at Cambes-en-Plaine at some time between the late afternoon of the 7th June and the evening of the 9th June 1944 while they were in the hands of the 1st Battalion of the 25th Panzergrenadier Regiment, 12th SS Hitlerjugend, their commanding officer at that time, who was witnessed in the area, being Hanz Waldmüller who was himself under the command of Kurt Meyer, who stated under oath and to a Court that he inspected and issued orders to Waldmüller at that location during

that relevant time.

If four Ulster Riflemen among the list of those killed at Cambes were murdered, then what was done about it? More importantly, who were they?

The answer to each of those questions is neither straightforward nor conclusive. The extensive enquiries and investigative work carried out by Colonels MacDonald and Boraston, along with the others in their SHAEF team, were confined under a term of reference to Canadian cases and to alleged atrocities which took place within the 9th Canadian Infantry Brigade area of operations. The 9th Canadian Infantry Brigade was one of three Brigades forming the 3rd Canadian Division. To confuse matters and complicate lines of communication they had on the extreme of their left flank the 2nd Battalion Royal Ulster Rifles who were part of the British 9th Infantry Brigade, in turn part of the British 3rd Infantry Division. Both identically numbered Divisions and within them, identically-numbered Brigades were assigned adjoining areas of the Normandy battlefield north of Caen. The originally defined boundary marking the Canadian/British divide ran through the western edge of the village of Cambes En Plaine. Technically, the village of Anisy, from where the 2nd RUR launched their attack on the 9th June, was within the Canadian area. To confuse matters further the operational boundary of the 12th SS Division ended at the railway line that ran north to south along the eastern edge of Cambes-en-Plaine. To the east of this line the 21st Panzer Division had operational control. There was therefore a section of the map at Cambes a few hundred yards wide that fell outside the terms of reference of the SHAEF enquiry but within which the 12th SS operated, notably the 1st Battalion of the 25th Panzer Grenadier Regiment.

If we step back and look at the map in broad terms, we can see how Royal Ulster Rifles prisoners were treated differently by the actions of the different German army units they faced, Waffen SS or Heer (Regular German Army). East of the River Orne,

in particular around St. Honorine, we know that when the 1st (Airborne) RUR men returned to the village after their initial battle on the 7th June they found that the Germans had actually buried their dead with respect in marked graves. The majority of their missing turned up at later dates in prisoner of war camps. West of the Orne the 2nd Battalion found their wounded murdered and left in an open trench. There is evidence that three men were taken prisoner; two of them Corporal McGovern and Rifleman Haslett were later found in prisoner of war camps and one, Trooper Fred Walker of the East Riding Yeomanry, was never seen again.

From recently released files in the British National Archive at Kew there is evidence that some sort of investigation had taken place in relation to an incident at Cambes. In a report written by the British Field Investigation Section of the War Crimes Group for North West Europe dated the 16th August 1948 a list of cases against the 12th SS Hitlerjugend that were not being proceed with and closed was compiled. The main criteria considered in closing these cases was generally the lack of witness evidence. [11]One case, with a legal section brief dated 6th July 1946, is headed 'CAMBES/ANISY'. Beneath the heading under a 'Remarks' section is the following text:

'This case has already been closed with legal section. The case concerns the killing of 15–20 prisoners of war on 8th June 1944 probably by members of the 5th Company II Battalion 25 Panzer Grenadier Regiment. The principal witness and soldier who was quoted as having taken part in this killing is reported by the Americans to have died in captivity. Difficulties were encountered during investigations in this case owing to the fact that witnesses confused this case with that of Chateau D' Audrieu owing probably to the similarity in the number of victims. No evidence was obtainable on which any particular member of the unit concerned could be charged with participation.'

---

11 The National Archives, WO 311/689, 'Report by Field Investigation Section, War Crimes Group (NWE) on Category III Cases, 12 SS Panzer Division.

There are no further details on this file to give an indication as to what the case specifically referred to. It can be seen from the report that an element of confusion across boundaries existed. We know, of course, that Cambes is where the four murdered men of the RUR were found. On the 8th of June Anisy was in the hands of the Allies and in fact was used as forming up point for the attack on Cambes on the 9th of June. The fact that the number of prisoners killed is reported as '15–20' begs questioning. Was it either 15 or was it 20? When we consider that four Riflemen were found shot through the head at Cambes plus one ERY Trooper was seen being led away in captivity it can be seen how the difference between 15 and 20 could be made up by adding the numbers of men murdered there plus the missing Trooper. Unfortunately, the file appears to have been 'weeded' and there are no documents attached which might have explained the detail.

Another file held at the National Archives[12], only just released for public viewing in 2021, contains correspondence between the British Judge Advocate General (JAG) and the Officer Commanding the 1 Canadian War Crimes Unit dated 10th July 1945. The file is headed, 'Shooting of British Prisoners of War by Germans belonging to 12 SS Panzer Division (Hitlerjugend) in Normandy, 7 – 21.6.44'. The file cover heading specifically relates to British prisoners of war and not Canadian or even Allied. On opening the file, the covering report sheet reads:

GERMAN WAR CRIMES
Alleged Crime: Murder
Against Whom Committed: British PW (prisoners of war)
Place: Normandy
Date of Offence: June 1944
Victims: Unknown

---

12 The National Archives, WO311/69 'Shooting of British POW by Germans Belonging to 12 SS Panzer Division (Hitler-Jugend) in Normandy 7 – 21.6.44.'

Names of Perpetrators with units and ranks:
Personnel of 12 S.S. Division
Brief Facts Of The Case:
As the majority of the victims were Canadians,
the cases were passed to them.

Again, as with the previous report, no specific details were
included in the file. A copy of the SHAEF Inquiry findings relating
to Kurt Meyer was however attached to it. With regards to the
cases at Cambes no specific investigation file can be found. That
does not mean that one doesn't exist but as things stand it appears
that the investigation into what took place at Cambes may have
been passed to the Canadians for inclusion in their case. At that
point it appears to have been dropped due to lack of eyewitness
evidence. Unfortunately, what took place there did so behind a
wall and in a village that had been cleared of all civilians and at a
time during which all British soldiers had withdrawn.

As to the identity of the four Royal Ulster Riflemen who were
murdered at Cambes we have no written record naming them or
that categorises them differently from the original list of casualties.
It appears though that their details were passed through the British
9th Infantry Brigade Headquarters. The dispatch rider with the
East Riding Yeomanry, Joseph Priestly made another entry in his
diary which was dated 7th June 1944[13]:

'June 7th Wed D2 Paratroops bring in 100 prisoners up from Caen
canal, snipers are giving us some trouble, 2 in church tower, tanks
shoot them out, gliders came in last night with supplies for airborne,
we advance into Cazelle this afternoon, held up at Periers Sur Le Dan
by snipers PBI (Poor Bloody Infantry?) shift them, gunned from the
air by ME 109 very close shave that time. 88mm are giving tanks some
trouble, Jerry shot some of our lads taken prisoner, he will pay for that.'

---

13 Joseph B Priestly, 'Diary of a soldier of the East Riding Yeomanry' Priestly
family collection, courtesy Mr. S Carr, Australia.

This entry was written on the 7th June with the obviously relevant last line 'Jerry shot some of our lads taken prisoner, he will pay for that.' Although we now know from the interviews of Richard Keegan and Stanley Burrows that it is believed that the prisoners were taken on the 7th, or that the wounded men were certainly left on that date it was not known for certain that they had been shot until the 9th, when Cambes was finally taken. Only then could Priestly have found this out. Either the entry was not written up by Priestly until after the 9th of June or the final line was added then after his original 7th June comments. Joseph Priestly's position in the battalion as a dispatch rider is significant. He wrote later that he accompanied the Commanding Officer on various duties and it may have been the case that he was privy to messages sent from the front lines to Brigade Headquarters and carried by him. He also confirms that the East Riding Yeomanry advanced to Cazelle on the 7th June. This was also the location of the 9th Brigade Headquarters, confirmed from their war diary entries covering the period. If, for instance, a post mortem examination were to be carried out by a Medical Officer to confirm the cause of death then this would be where it would have taken place. Again, unfortunately no records of such examinations can be found. What can be stated for certain is that the bodies of four of those killed on the 7th June were treated differently from the others killed on that date.

Of the 43 men killed in the fighting for Cambes between the 7th and 9th of June 1944, the bodies of 39 of them were originally buried in the village itself, either at the eastern edge of the village just north of where the railway halt building can be seen today or where the Commonwealth War Graves Cemetery is today. Between mid-May and early June 1945 all of the bodies were exhumed and concentrated into what would become permanent Commonwealth War Graves Cemeteries, cemeteries where their graves can be seen today. There are nine graves of men from the 2nd Battalion The Royal Ulster Rifles in Cambes-en-Plaine

Military Cemetery which is situated close to the where the gap in the wall surrounding Cambes was in June 1944. The remaining graves were moved to La Delivrande War Cemetery approximately four miles north of Cambes. The details of the original burial locations however can be seen on grave concentration reports held by the Commonwealth War Graves Commission and can be read online. These reports typically show the name, rank, number and regiment of each soldier along with exhumation date and the grid reference of the original burial location along with the details of the final burial location. Significantly the bodies of four men were not originally buried at Cambes village.[14] From their concentration reports we can see that they were all buried together at a grid reference just south of the village of Cazelle, the location of the 9th Infantry Brigade Headquarters at that time, the same location from where the dispatch rider Priestly operated from. The four men buried at that location were:

Corporal Ernest John ROGERS 7017531
Rifleman Robert James MULLAN 7021305
Rifleman Henry J. VALENTINE 7016349
Rifleman Michael P. MICHAELIDES 7020577

On the exhumation report the dates of death for two of these men had been altered, both Michaelides and Mullan were initially recorded as being killed on the 8th June 1944. This date was changed in red ink to the 9th June 1944 so all four have the date of death recorded as the 9th June 1944. When we look at the record made by Sergeant Drumgoole[15], the medical sergeant, the dates differ. In this record he recorded the death of Michaelides and Valentine as having taken place on the 7th June. Michaelides'

---

14 CWGC Grave Concentration Report, www.cwgc.org/find-records/find-war-dead/casualty-details/2340176/ernest-john-rogers/#&gid=2&pid=1 accessed 24 Nov 2023.

15 James Drumgoole Papers, '2nd Bn Casualties, D-Day' Royal Ulster Rifles Museum, Bedford Street, Belfast.

name is the first of the four to be recorded and he initially wrote the word 'Dead' and then wrote over the entry with the word 'Killed'. Rifleman Valentine's name was entered immediately after Michaelides' and again recorded as 'Killed' both men have 'Sharapnel' recorded against their names. Sergeant Drumgoole recorded the death of Corporal Rogers on the 8th June 1944 and again the words 'Shrapnel' and 'Killed' are next to his name. There was no record made in his notes for Rifleman Mullan. For the location of the casualty for all of his notes made for the 7th and 8th of June he entered 'Wood, Gazelle'. It is only for those entries made for the 9th June that he changed this and entered his casualty details as 'Cambes'. Drumgoole's notes appear initially to be contemporaneous however for casualties recorded after the 8th June they have been placed in alphabetical order, indicating that from that date at any rate they were not recorded as the men were observed or treated. The dates of death of these four men were recorded on the Roll of Honour contained within the official Regimental History; Valentine, Mullan and Rogers on the 9th of June and Michaelides this time recorded as having been killed on the 8th.

A further record was made relating to Riflemen Michaelides and Valentine by Captain Ryan who had been wounded and evacuated on the 9th of June. He had retained the list he had made of the original landing craft deployments for the Headquarters and Support Companies. From this list we can tell that Michaelides and Valentine were stretcher-bearers. Against both of their names he had written the word 'Dead' in pencil. This note must have been made on the 9th after he entered Cambes as he was evacuated wounded on that date. This is an indication, although far from conclusive that he saw them, dead. With the knowledge that both these men were stretcher-bearers' weight can be added to a theory that they were wounded while attempting to extricate two other wounded men from the wood, all four then becoming casualties. Sergeant Drumgoole of course would have

known them as they were under his direct command and perhaps made his own enquiries before recording their deaths on the 7th of June. He still could not have known their fate until the 9th. It certainly appears that regardless of all of the different dates of death that were recorded the Directorate of Graves Registration and Enquiry applied the date of death of the 9th June 1944 for each of the four men originally buried at Cazelle. On the grave registration document[16], a further reference number was written against each of their names, again in red pen, SSP/C/NWE/1309. No corresponding file can be found for this number either in the National Archives or with the Commonwealth War Graves Commission. One can probably be safe to assume that the 'C' and 'NWE' stand for Calvados and North West Europe respectively, indicating the theatre of operations in Normandy; the number obviously denotes a specific file from that group of files but with regard to the initial letters 'SS' and 'P' one can only hazard a guess.

On those four men whom I have named as possible victims of murder I would like to quote from Ian Campbell's 1996 work on the Abbaye d'Ardenne atrocity 'Murder at the Abbaye'[17] which dealt with those Canadian victims of the 12th SS Hitlerjugend. He wrote:

'Today, there are very few wives or siblings of these twenty men left in the world to remember them... A couple of the murdered men had children; few of these children were old enough to remember their dads. But these twenty men, who went away to that war over half a century ago, were very real people. They were extraordinarily ordinary and total unremarkable men... Nevertheless, they were men with dreams and aspirations. They loved and were loved.

16 CWGC Grave Concentration Report, www.cwgc.org/find-records/find-war-dead/casualty-details/2340176/ernest-john-rogers/#&gid=2&pid=1 accessed 24 Nov 2023.

17 Ian J Campbell, 'Murder at the Abbaye: The Story of Twenty Canadian Soldiers Murdered at the Abbaye D'Ardenne', Golden Dog Press, 15 Aug. 2000.

They lived, they served, and they were murdered while doing their duty. And today, all Canadians owe them something, if it is only to remember that they were once with us, that they did their duty to the best of their capabilities, and that they were murdered on the grounds at the Abbaye in a faraway place. Their deaths were tragic, but to forget them, or to remember them only as faceless statistics, is more tragic still.'

I have borrowed and printed these words from author and historian Mr. Ian Campbell. He wrote them to describe how he believes we should feel regarding the murder of those Canadian soldiers at the Abbaye d'Ardenne on the 7th June 1944. His words cut through differences of opinion and politics and moral argument and highlight what I believe should be the thoughts of right-thinking people, those belonging to a civilised society. Ian wrote of the murder of twenty men, whose names we know and who lie today at Bazenville, Bény-sur-Mer and Bretteville-sur-laize cemeteries in Normandy and indeed are respectfully remembered by Canada. Those who know me and who have kindly played devil's advocate to my thoughts will understand how I have laboured long with the idea of naming those who I believe were murdered on the 7th June 1944 at Cambes. For eighty years the actual fact that they were murdered at all was lost to that convenient phrase, 'the fog of war'. Nevertheless, these four men had volunteered to fight to preserve and defend the actual civilisation that allows me to make this case, and equally allows you, as reader, the freedom to agree with or to dismiss entirely, or for that matter, to challenge my findings as you see fit. In fact, those murdered deserve no less than that level of scrutiny. They had fought their way through the wall at the village of Cambes to confront an enemy that was as evil as they were courageous. Once wounded and rendered incapable of being a threat to anyone, they in effect surrendered their liberty and at that point should have been afforded, at the very least, the right to life. Of the sixteen men

known to have been killed that day I can say with certainty that four were murdered in cold blood and twelve were killed in action. One could calculate odds on whether those named are correct or not against the list of all killed; to do so would show them the greatest disrespect. In contrast I have come to my conclusions as outlined based on the extent of the information available today combined with the balance of probabilities.

To echo Ian Campbell's words, we have a duty to remember that these men were murdered, their deaths were tragic, but to forget them, or to remember them only as faceless statistics, is more tragic still. If I am wrong in my identification, I can only apologise to any who may be offended but I will welcome with heartfelt thanks any correction. I make no apologies however for calling out murder and for highlighting those who I most strongly believe were responsible.

8th September 1944
Basse-Bodeux, Belgium

[18] *'During the march back through Belgium, individual members of the Division were ambushed and murdered by partisans. On 8 September, Sturmbannführer Hanz Waldmüller and Untersturmführer Marquardt rode on a motorcycle with a sidecar from Werbomont to Stavelot. On a stretch of approximately six kilometres they had to cross through an extensive forest.*

At a spot where the road dropped off after crossing a hill down toward Basse-Bodeux, at a lower elevation, the partisans had positioned a cable across the road. When the cycle approached, they tightened the cable so that it came up off the ground. The cycle either stopped or was caught by the cable. The partisans opened fire. Soon after, several horse-drawn carriages of Sturmbannführer

---

18 Hubert Meyer, 'The 12th SS Vol. One – The History of the Hitler Youth Panzer Division' J.J. Fedorowicz Publishing Inc. 1994, Stockpole Books editions 2005, 2021.

Waldmüller reached that spot. The men observed the traces of the ambush with horror. Untersturmführer Marquardt sat dead on the rear seat of the cycle; he had been shot in the head. The driver was found, seriously wounded, in the undergrowth on the left side of the road. After a lengthy search, Sturmbannführer Waldmüller was discovered in the drainage pipe of a small lake. His body had been brutally mutilated, his belly had been slit open, the genitalia cut off. Both dead men and the wounded driver were taken along on one of the horse carriages.'

28th December 1945, 11.45hrs
Aurich, Germany

Major-General C. VOKES:
[19]'I declare the Court open…
(To the accused) Brigadeführer Kurt Meyer, the court has found you guilty of the First, Fourth, and Fifth Charges in the First Charge Sheet. The sentence of this Court is that you suffer death by being shot. The [findings] of guilty and the sentence are subject to confirmation. The proceedings are now closed.'

Kurt Meyer's death sentence was commuted to a sentence of life imprisonment on the 14th January 1946. He was freed from custody on the 7th September 1954 and died on the 23rd December 1961.

---

19 P Whitney Lackenbauer & Chris MV Madsen, 'Kurt Meyer on Trial, a Documentary Record' Canadian Defence Academy Press, 2007.

9

The Final Word

2003
Belfast, Northern Ireland

Hamilton LAWRENCE:
'We never broke out of Cambes Wood, there was no way
we were ever going to break out the way they wanted to.
Then the plans were changed, they withdrew the Brigade
back for a rest, two days it was; only two days to regroup
and then we were going to take Caen. When we left one
of the other regiments took over, the (South Staffordshire)
Regiment because our Brigade had to go to Caen. They
took over there and that is all their graveyard that is there
now. They kept them there to keep the enemy thinking
that we were still there you see. They took us back and we
regrouped and we went a different way to Caen, the whole
Brigade. We managed to get right round Cambes and by-
pass it altogether. The enemy wasn't expecting that with
the other battalion being there. They thought we were still
defensive and they didn't realise that we were going to take
a flanker off them there and we got out to the outside of
Caen. It was all open of course then, no shelter or anything
there. We just took wee villages as we went along. That was
our objective from day one, from D-Day, we were to take
Caen.

We got onto this hill, the enemy had good defences there

and the artillery couldn't knock their outposts (observation posts) out, at Colombelles there were two big chimney stacks and they could see over the whole plain (from them). The planes couldn't bomb them, they were too small for the planes to bomb them and they were too far away for the artillery to hit them. So we got onto the hill the night before and we got onto the high ground and we could look into Caen and we could see the big outposts and all. We were on the hill and we watched the bombers come over and they bombarded it all night long, everything, no matter what got hit. To see them all going over, I wouldn't have liked to have been there, we were thinking more of the people that were there, how in the name those people lived through that with the destruction going on the whole night long. It stopped when daylight came, knowing we had to go in to attack. Nobody knew what to expect going in there.

At day break we sent a patrol in and the patrol couldn't get in, there was nowhere to walk! Everything was holed and muddled up. They managed to get down and get into the centre of Caen but came back again because they couldn't get any support or anything. Anyway, they were the first platoon into Caen, the Recce (Platoon). Then the next morning we got organised then, we could get no support, no Bren Gun Carriers, nothing like that there, so we were told it just had to be the infantry that went in and we had to go more or less street fighting. That was what it was then and it was mostly sniper fire then because the enemy had gone to the other side of the Orne River. It got tough then because it was all sniping. You didn't know where you were going, especially when we got in to near the centre of Caen, and the big outposts, the observation posts, they were still there and we had a bit of a job getting in then. We managed to get into the centre of the town. It was great, where I was I was up at one of the big castles in there and we could see away to a big church, down a big avenue. My position was with the Bren Gun and I had a couple with me and the rest of

the section and platoon were on the other side of the street. We had to go all the way along this big avenue to the centre, the big church and the castle. We had to make our way the whole way up that, house by house and door by door. When you were on one side you had to watch the other side of the street for any snipers, then you had to root them out. Some of the people were living in the houses and they knew the people was upstairs, that the enemy was there and they warned you, to give you a signal to look up. You had to go street by street, no support, just walking in, an individual, just one or two people and the whole Company had to go along each side of the street, and that was only one bit of it. There were no mines, just unexploded bombs, you didn't know where the (sniping) was coming from but the main ones were coming from the church, they had a machine gun covering us from up there and mortar bombs to fire right along the street from there. Our main objective was to get that place, the outpost, because it looked right over the River Orne and all, it covered the whole place so our main objective was to get up there, no matter what happened along that street.

I came round a corner of shops and I had the Bren gun and my pal sat down beside me and we just got around the corner and the sniper fire came down from the church around me. They were in the shops and houses as well. We didn't know what to expect but we were lucky enough to have met the Free French people, the Underground people and they took us in, into the town and all of the people came out then. If we hadn't have had those people to take us in we wouldn't have known where we were. They took our flag and cheered all up the street. We had to go straight through. It really was a bad mess, it was mad. The only thing standing really was the church.

When we went in there was nothing. The rubble was all over the roads, no roads or anything, there was nothing. You were lucky to get walking in there but you couldn't get

any transport, no bicycle, nothing. No people about, empty. All you were getting was sniper fire and machine gun fire. You didn't see any of the enemy because they were all in houses and all. All the shops, everything was in ruins. You could picture how lovely it was before, Caen a capital city and it was small, it didn't take much to blow the whole lot to bits with them bombers. We don't know how the people survived in it. All the dead bodies and people lying about the rubble never got cleared away, you were tramping over peoples bodies and children, everything, animals, dogs, anything at all that was there was blown away to bits. No medical supplies, no hospital or nothing, it was really bad.

We were glad that we got in there and enemy was away, the people knew they were liberated then. We were surprised at the people coming out, waving flags, giving them drinks and all, it was amazing, I didn't expect that, holding your hand and shaking hands and all.

As soon as we took our objective (the church) our direction was the River Orne, the Company was to go straight on, we weren't to go into Caen, into Caen but not into the centre. Our main objective, we got. Although we didn't take it in a day everybody was pleased, even Montgomery himself, we got a good report from him saying how pleased he was that although it took a long time we took our objective and it made a difference to the war. That was how they were able to get the break around the River Orne and through the Falaise Gap. When we were on the river (Orne) it was peace and quiet, we knew the enemy were away on the other side and had disappeared altogether. We were able to get food and somewhere to stay in the villages there outside Caen, it was a relief for us to get it all over but we felt sorry for the people we left behind inside Caen.

All I remember about Caen was when I went back again, to remember what I had seen and then to remember when I had went back on the 50th anniversary, what it was like then, when I got the medal and they told me to come over.

They were so pleased, I had a map and the Mayor was looking at it and I explained and he saw what we had done, The Ulster Rifles. He was that pleased that he said "Was there anything special you want to see?" I said to him yes, I want to go back to Cambes and at that he said it will be very difficult to get to Cambes because the whole area was surrounded by troops and police because The Queen was there. He called his son and his chauffeur and he told his son to take this man to Cambes. We got stopped three or four times by road blocks by the police and all and they had to show who they were and who was this in the back, me with my medals and my badge and uniform, they said all right let him go. But when I got in there, he left me and said to go and look around. I was disappointed when I seen it. Where were the soldiers that were killed? Where were they buried? They weren't in Cambes Wood.

I have a lot of time, I watch a lot of documentaries on TV and you see all of these photos of the D-Day landings. I've never seen one boat, not one boat with the Ulster Rifles on it at all. We never seen any reporters, didn't see any reporters from the *Daily Telegraph* or anything. No one came to speak to you. It was never reported really and that's why whenever we came home nobody knew anything about it. I've found that my nephews and friends and all knew nothing. They didn't know anything about what we'd done, Caen? They wouldn't even know we were the first to get into it. Even the battles, they didn't know how many people were killed or anything, amazing. You hear the stories about everybody else, it's amazing, even the 1st Battalion, there's not much mentioned about them.

It's very important for the Ulster Rifles to get the story out now, no one knows, it wasn't to have been allowed in the British Army, for two regular Battalions of one Regiment to fight side by side, you weren't allowed to do that. With the Ulster Rifles two battalions fought side by side, at Pegasus Bridge and at Cambes, no one knows anything about that.

Although they were in two different Divisions they were fighting side by side. It's a shame that there's nothing written about them at all.

I just want to be remembered just the same as everybody else because I wasn't the only one. It's amazing to go right through the fighting the whole way, as Montgomery said 'From D-Day to VE Day' the whole way, we were in attack the whole time. No breaks, right through to Bremen. I'm very pleased with myself to have come through it but I feel for the other ones who didn't come through it. Cambes Wood wasn't the worst, the next objective was Troarn and although we didn't lose as many men the battle for Troarn was worse. We never captured Troarn, that was one of the objectives we never took, because we couldn't get there.

No, no, no way. I'm no hero. Not a hero going out and blowing a tank up or rescuing other people, no way. I just done what I had to do and survived it. That was my main objective, survival.'

James BOWDEN:

'We saw these planes coming over our heads and we knew Caen was about three miles away from where we were. We saw the mass coming over, the next thing we saw was the German anti-aircraft guns opening up and they had the sky plastered with the black smoke all over the place. Those fellows went straight through and we got the glasses (binoculars) out and we were looking at the planes it was just on the edge of darkness, near dusk and actually we could see the bombs dropping on Caen. With the guns and that you could feel the ground shaking under your feet. I could feel that, a sort of a shudder. We saw them coming back. I did see one of those bombers coming back with a hole six or seven feet long and about four feet wide, half of it's wing shot away, and he was heading for England. I often wonder if that fella got home or not, or did he come down, I don't know. I don't know what the casualties were there but they

pounded Caen very hard, no doubt about it. There was over a hundred bombers there. They wrecked the place. There was hardly a building left standing, except the Cathedral. I didn't see it because we never went near Caen but the Ulster Rifles did. The second Battalion of the Ulster Rifles, they can tell you about what Caen looked like, I didn't see Caen until it was rebuilt, forty odd years afterwards. We were on the other side and when the breakout from the bridgehead took place, we moved along the coast through to Cabourg, Deauville along there up to Le Havre.

People say war is hell, It's hell right enough because it's not normal. I mean you're killing people you don't know and you're shooting, it's not real, you haven't got time to be scared, you're there to survive and do what you're asked to do, what you need to do and that's it. You never know from one minute to the next whether you're going to live or die. I was very fortunate, I didn't see bodies that were blown to bits, I saw bodies that had been hit and wounded and shrapnel and all that. I didn't see... like Bloody Friday, what the Police saw on Bloody Friday, bodies being blown to bits and all that, I never saw that at all.

I did nothing, compared to what people did you know. There were heroes, but then of course a lot of heroes were mad men. There were times when you had to get up and do something, other times you got your head down. I kept my head down when I had to keep it down. Most of what was coming at me was shelling and mortars and I couldn't see who was throwing the stuff at me at all. Most of the people in the army that I know are dead. They'll not remember me. Those who will remember me will be my daughters and nephews and that. I would say I'm nearly a nobody, not worth thinking about, when I consider and read about these people who I consider brave. There were thousands like me. I was a survivor. I was there, I was there on that one great day in history, and I jumped into it, one of the first.'

Richard KEEGAN:

'The men, whenever they were killed the Clergymen that were there would have given them a sort of a burial service, there's no two ways about it. A bit of a cross with their name stuck on it. Once things got more organised they were dug up then and given a proper burial. It made you feel bloody awful when you heard of a man being buried at the side of a road or anything like that, it made you feel terrible. That's not a way to treat a soldier. But then when you seen what was done at the bitter end it made a different picture altogether. As I see it now it is something that should be respected for time immemorial, there's no two ways about it. Young people that are coming up today, if they can be brought to that part of the country and see these things, it would do them the world of good and make them appreciate. Maybe their grandfather is one of them, maybe their great grandfather is one of them but it should be something that is brought home to everybody. This is something that happened that if the World had been a better place it wouldn't have happened, but when it did happen and the men went out and fought for what was right, then it was worthwhile, even they were killed, wounded, lost limbs and all the rest of it, it was at the bitter end worthwhile because it sort of made a better place for us to live in.

I don't think that the Ulster Riflemen are remembered enough. No, I would say here in Northern Ireland it's not a big deal, it's not a big deal, but yet whenever you go out to France and you see the children putting flowers on the graves then it makes you think what our ones are doing at home, whenever they wouldn't even put a memorial up. There's not a memorial I know of anywhere in Northern Ireland. There should be memorials, the 11th of November is Remembrance Day but I also say that in the summertime there should be another Remembrance Day for the Second World War. I feel hurt, very hurt.

Whenever I go, don't put an obituary in the paper, get me

out of the house and into the ground as quick as you can. I don't look at myself as a hero in the sense of bravado, but I still say that we were all heroes, because we took part in doing the job. We tried to do the job.'

Robert LOUGHLIN:
'You see that much, it should never happen, countries fighting against each other and fellas getting murdered, I don't agree with it. Where does it get them? Nowhere, only a loss of life. I don't agree with wars, no. A knock comes to your door and the postman gives you an aul brown pasteboard thing, sealed up to say your son has been killed in action, that's it. I don't agree with it, no. If you seen those young fellas lying dead when we landed. They landed and in the next two minutes they were lying in France there dead, they never even seen it.

On D-Day the two Battalions were good Battalions. We lost a lot of men too. Not as many as the crossing of the Rhine. You think anybody would remember me? I don't mind, I have my own way of going and I have my own memories. If I were to meet somebody who was in the same position as me I could have a great conversation. It would be very serious.'

Martin VANCE:
'I think it was absolutely marvellous really that such a force went in the way they did. I don't think there was and I don't think there will ever be in my lifetime again anything like that ever to happen again. Really, something to be very proud of, to say 'I was there'. I feel very proud to have been there with my comrades, my mates and that, so many of us together even yet we're very very good friends. In my own right I suppose I was no more a hero than any of the rest of the lads. I felt certainly good. We were all heroes put it that way, every man that took part in it. Every man. It's hard to say how I would want to be remembered, just that I was

there. I took part in that and feel very, very proud.

What you can see in most of these documentaries is all about the English regiments, and I'm not taking anything away from them, we had nobody to put our case forward for us. It's nice to see that you (film makers) are doing something to correct that. I would like the people to know the part that we played and I would like the people to know what the part of the Royal Irish Fusiliers and the Royal Inniskillings played. The Irish regiments in general weren't really recognised as they should have been.

Colonel CHARLEY[1] is the man for putting our case forward for us, a gentleman. School children and people really don't know who the Royal Ulster Rifles are. You hear about the Royal Irish Regiment but thats a combination of about five or six regiments but we were the Regiments who got the honours and the colours. The Royal Ulster Rifles, they were a glorious regiment and always will be and it is important that people in Northern Ireland and Ireland in general let them know who they are and what they done. That's very, very important. People say 'The Royal Ulster Rifles? Who are they?' And that's very hurting. I hope this goes out and lets people know who they are, what they

---

1   Colonel Robin Charley OBE, KstJ, JP, DL (1924-2019) enlisted with The Royal Ulster Rifles in 1943. He was commissioned as an officer in 1945. He served in Palestine, Egypt, Korea, Japan, Hong Kong, Germany, Australia, and the UK. On 1st July 1968, The Royal Ulster Rifles, amalgamated with two other regiments to form The Royal Irish Rangers, which Colonel Charley served in until 1971. From 1972–1989, he held the job of Regimental Secretary of The Royal Irish Rangers together with that of Secretary of The Royal Ulster Rifles Association and Curator of The Royal Ulster Rifles Museum. These roles meant he had a great deal of contact with RUR veterans. Colonel Charley knew Marty Vance, Billy McConnell, and Sam Lowry particularly well, as they had all served together with 1RUR in the Korean War. Until he passed in July 2019 aged 95 years, Colonel Charley remained loyal to his veterans and their concerns taking on trusteeships and other positions with The Northern Ireland War Memorial, The Royal Ulster Rifles Museum, The Royal Ulster Rifles Association, The Somme Association, The Not Forgotten Association, SSAFA, and The Forces Help Society.

are and what they did and the lives that people gave for their freedom. Most important, the old saying 'They gave their today for your tomorrow', that's very true and people should remember that. Colonel Charley does his very best to put this over.'

Sam LOWRY:

'I really don't look back unless somebody raises it. Mentally the old brain ticks over and puts it in the background until something happens to bring it forward and then it's with sorrow and remorse. The dead, you can't do anything to help them, or the wounded, well you can help them still. You put it in the background, you keep it in your head. Sometimes I think I made history and I read about it. Other times I think I wish I had stayed in the aircraft factory! You look back with pride maybe in certain cases but the pride is for what? That you blew up a place or you wrecked a place or you killed someone. Maybe my philosophy is all wrong, but that's the way I feel at times. We in Ulster do not blow our own trumpets. If you look at the industrial civilian side, I mean Ferguson, Dunlop tyres, many, many different things. There are men out in that street I'm sure and if we went out and asked them (about war) they would say 'Hey, forget it'. So many things happen in wartime that shouldn't. I get very annoyed, today I happened to get talking to a young student and I mentioned the Korean War and they had no idea that the British played a part in it. When I look back in my own life and think of 1914–18 all I knew was in say, 1936 or '37, all I knew was that they had a parade at the Cenotaph and there were a load of dead men. I think it's a lot about publicity. It's a failing. There's misuse of the word hero. I think it's a thing that was handed out ad-lib. I would just like to be remembered to my family, that Sam passed this way.'

Bill McCONNELL:

'I came through it, yes. When I go back it brings back a lot of memories, I go back to see my friends, the graves of the friends that I had and boys that I come up through the army with and people who I didn't know. In them days you hardly knew anyone out of another company. The only people you knew, or even when you went to the canteen back at barracks, 'A' Company would have went in at ten to ten and you were out again at ten past and another company went in but you didn't get to know any of the other company. I didn't even know the names, the only reason why I knew Bobby Stevenson was that Bobby was a friend of mine. You didn't know who was who and this is the way it was kept.

I can still see them sometimes when you've been out and had a few jars at night. Your memory plays tricks on you and you go back to the same ways. I've woken up many a morning with a cold sweat. Those things, and the glider landing. Most things that affect me more is the Rhine crossing more so than in France.

I would have loved to have gone in on the glider with the Ox and Bucks and I would have loved to have seen the Ulster Rifles going into the bridge as well. It would have been great. Not taking anything away from the 52nd, no way. The 52nd Ox and Bucks and the Rifles, as a couple of them put it to me, we were cousins because wherever the Ox and Bucks went the Rifles went. During the war in France we done leap-frog. They took a place we went through them, we took a place and they went through us and it was only us and them. We never saw the 12th Devons, at all. They were supposed to be in our brigade but we never seen them. It was only the Ox and Bucks and the Rifles. We were very very close even back in camp and in barracks, even today. We done the crossing of The Rhine together, everywhere we went together, the two battalions.

But when I die my ashes are to be taken to Ranville Cemetery beside the Airborne Cross, not without

permission of course, but that's where I want it to be; scattered there. And it's been agreed with my family that they will take it there. I think I belong there with the boys that I know. Old friends, old mates, that's why, and this is written into my will, I want it that way. Just as simple as that and my family, they know when I'm cremated my ashes are to go there, hopefully. Well, I'll not be worrying about it.

So that's why I like seeing the Airborne Memorial for the remainder of my days. I just want to, some of my mates, most of my friends are buried there and I just want to be along with them. It's maybe an old man's fad but I've had this for years now and my family have been sort of a way growing up with that, which I wanted. You see I'm, all my life, most of my life I was a soldier, from I was 17 up until 1970.

I went back because I wanted to see the graves of all my friends who were killed there. And I wanted to see where they were buried. The bodies of ours that were killed were buried three times. They were buried where they fell then the bodies got lifted again and they were buried in another place, at Ranville, Ranville Cemetery, that was all changed. The farmer down at Longueval where the house is, they were buried in his front lawn and he wanted the bodies removed immediately so they had to get the bodies out of it. So it was only after 1946 when they did that, the Graves Commission took over. They were buried in makeshift, they were buried all right as they had, you know, no coffins. They were buried sewn up in their uniform, in their blanket and they were buried like that. Even now they are buried that way. And that's the reason why I go back. I go back and I can just see the faces or think I see the faces of the boys when I go to visit their grave, even when I was over there this year I can still see the faces of the people as I knew them, before they were killed. It's just young men, like I was myself, not an old man like I am now. It's just the same, they're not old, the faces are not old and they don't look any older… and then

they just disappear.

To me the cemeteries are very serene and very quiet. It is a different atmosphere to me, going into a grave yard where I know the people who I soldiered with are lying there. They are beautifully kept and well looked after. The arch at the cemetery at Bayeau is for the people who are still missing in action. They are ones which a lot of them we know to be killed except that there was no senior officer present so they are still down as missing in action. Bobby Stevenson's name is still on that. There's about five or six of ours whose names are on it which we know two or three of them were killed. There's ones missing which no-one has ever heard of. Often there were a lot of people that were killed and there were tanks run over the bodies, so they'll never be found. The identity discs; we found out that the asbestos identity discs we had, they burned. So afterwards we got the steel discs with the stamp on them. If a man is killed, the identity disc – there's three identity discs – one stays around his neck, there's one in a tin on the top of the grave and there's one is sent to records to certify the death. You see there was times they were burnt so there's no way of finding out who they were or what they were. I can just think about it… my mind just… I can see him (Bobby Stevenson) when he was standing beside me. If we were in the barrack room together and we're sitting having a joke or having a laugh or something like that, or we're having a cigarette. He's still there with me. At times you have to shake your head sometimes and forget about it, I can't. I don't think I ever will do. Just one of those things.

My brother in law, he used to say to me 'Bill, are you sure that yous were in France, because you're never mentioned'. It's absolutely true, and when I was at the reunion there was six of us there to meet the Prince of Wales at the opening of the museum there, and it was all Paras. The Ox and Bucks and the Rifles weren't even mentioned. There was a thing with RUR on it and he spoke to me and he asked was the

hotel accommodation all right, was the drink all right was the food all right and he shook hands with me and it was nice meeting him, but the men there were all Paras, but they weren't there, they weren't near Pegasus Bridge and it makes every one of the 6th Air Landing Brigade, the Ox and Bucks and ourselves, it makes us all bloody annoyed, and even with him there, and he is the Colonel in Chief of the Paras, they weren't interested in us at all. Words can't describe it, it's just unbelievable that you are just not mentioned. There was a couple of things in the *Belfast Telegraph* I think or something but I don't know, somebody would tell me. But there was more afterwards, after the war. But during the war there was very little. The people of Longueval are very great with the Ulster Rifles. Through the years from '96 to now we have always been made very welcome. The people of the village come out and join us and join us for drinks in the Marie afterwards and they like seeing the parade.

I'm not a hero, I joined the army to do a job. I enjoyed myself. I did thirty years, it was my life and I had to make it my life and I was just an ordinary infantryman. I was no hero, I done what I was told to do and nothing more up to that stage. Well, I was glad I went, If I hadn't I would have felt terrible because most of the people my age had already joined either one of the forces, either Navy, Army or Air Force. I would have felt out of place if I hadn't have been one of the ones that went as well. Just that. I don't think I did any more than anyone else. I don't think myself above anyone to do anything, to be remembered at all. My family will remember me and if they do that's all.'

Stanley BURROWS:

'I dream very regularly and I dream that I'm going through maybe not exactly the same kind of battle but I always dream that I'm going through some kind of a fight and there's shelling and all going on and all the rest, but in my dream I always find that I can't defend myself. Something's going to

happen to me and I can't defend myself. These dreams have been very regular over the years. Maybe too I would sit and meditate a lot about it and think back to the pals and I think of the good times we had together like Crangles and Bobby Beck, the BBC. I would think back on it and I would feel sad when I think of what happened and to realise that out of the lot of them that I went personally about with, that I'm the only one that's alive today at 81 years of age. I would see (their faces) Crangles very very plainly, I would see Bobby Beck and I would see some of the men like Scotty who was actually hit and wounded. Sometimes it comes to me when I see him lying there and I try to get that image out of my head and I try to get the one where we were running about together as young soldiers going around the sing-songs and the various things we did.

On the 17th June 1944 I had been on these old hardy rations all this time and with all these old hard biscuits my stomach was a bit hard going so I had slipped out and I managed to catch a chicken and kill it. I brought the chicken back and I had an old biscuit tin and I put the chicken in and got some goose-gabs and a couple of leeks and that's all I could get. So I put them in and I thought we'd have goose-gab soup with the leeks in it and the chicken. When I was cooking it some shells came over and petrol was let off. The petrol was hit and exploded and it went all round my face and my hands. I jumped up from where it had happened and I heard someone shout 'throw water over it' well I knew water wasn't a good thing for petrol and I ran forward and dived down into another trench and threw the muck all over my face to smother the flames. I stood up and the next minute a couple of men had jumped on my back and pushed me down again. I didn't know but my neck was still burning. The helmet saved my hair and the camouflage on it was on fire, they pushed the helmet off and they managed to smother the flames.

I made a mistake again, not being a hero but I didn't

let the first aid come up to me. I was all red and smarting very badly, my face and my hands and I decided to stay in the trench for the night. During the night I lay there and I was shivering with cold, I think I was in shock. When morning came I looked at my hands and they were covered in blisters, I couldn't open my hands. I was shaking badly and my face was a mass of blisters. One of the men right off the reel got the medics up to me and I was bandaged all over my head with just wee slots for my eyes and my mouth and my hands were bandaged. The medics got me up and got me out. They were flying some of the worst men home and I was amongst them. Now these bombers that were flying me home had been bringing troops in so they couldn't put a red cross on them. When I got into the plane I was walking wounded, they put us into the big bomber. When we were flying over our own convoy when we were out to sea, we couldn't fly to the right or to the left as the Germans would have got us there so we thought that the safest thing to do was to fly over the Navy, which you weren't allowed to do. They opened fire, the Royal Navy opened fire at us on the plane and all you could see was a big puff of smoke at each side and a 'woof' and you could feel the plane shake. One of the co-pilots came in and said 'Don't worry, it's our own.' Somebody on the plane shouts up 'What do they think they're trying to do? They're trying to hit us. It's worse getting shot by your own after getting this far'. We managed to get out and they flew us to England. So inside a week or two I had been fired at on land, I had been fired at at sea on the ship, going through the hull, and now I'd been fired at in the air, and they missed me every time. It was lovely to look down and see such a fleet of arms but it was terrifying to look out and see these shells bursting at each side of your plane and to think 'Now I'm out of it, I'm going to get killed by our own troops'. That wasn't a very nice feeling.

I had a great loyalty towards Crangles my mate, I didn't want to leave him. I didn't want to go. I thought maybe by

the morning I'd be all right if I stayed the night and stayed with my old pal Crangles.

When I went into hospital the WAAF'S were girls who met you coming off the planes. They met you and carried the stretchers and took us into the hospital. I was sitting at the end of the bed and these WAAF's were going around giving cigarettes to us all. This girl came over and spoke to me and asked me where I came from, I said I came from Loopland in Belfast. She said 'Oh, I knew a wee sailor from there'. I said what was his name and she said 'Geoff Burrows'. I said well that is my brother and I don't know whether he is dead or alive, I just heard his ship was blown up. She told me he was still alive and she said 'You wait there and I'll get you some extra cigarettes.' She went away and I was sitting on the end of the bed and a doctor came to me and said that because I was burns I would have to go to another hospital. So, just then the ambulance arrived and I was sitting in the back of the ambulance and this girl came up and threw the cigarettes into the back. That was the last I seen of the girl, but she told me my brother was still alive.

In spite of being wounded, a lot of people were glad to get out of it, some soldiers never wanted to ever go back, but I don't know what was in me, I couldn't tell you what it was but I had an awful feeling that I wanted to be back with the Ulster Rifles and back with them again. I knew that my mother like all good mothers do their best to stop me, and she had written to Major Tighe-Wood. He wrote and told her that no way would he get out as quick as that, there was a whole procedure that you must go through before you go back out to France. He had been wounded after me and he was waiting to get out. Inside me there was an awful desire to get back. I don't know what it was, there was some loyalty to my comrades, there was something inside me wanted to be with them again. I couldn't tell you why, maybe I was half crazy but I just wanted to be back out there again. I got back out, only to be wounded a second time.

I was in hospital and the Medical Officer of the hospital wrote to my mother and told her exactly what was wrong with me. A letter arrived and in it she told me then that Crangles had been killed and that was very, very sad for me to hear that, very sad. Knowing that he had already two of his family killed. It was very hard to take. Here was somebody you've soldiered with all these years and now he was killed and what happened? That was one of the reasons why I was anxious to get back, to see if I could get any details about where he was and where he was buried and all the rest.

When I went back (to Cambes) first I had this awful image of the way they were buried, just wrapped in a ground sheet and a blanket and put in the ground. That image was always with me for forty years. When I went back on the fortieth anniversary and saw the lovely graves and the way they were tended to and the way they were looked after a big burden had left me. Here I was the same now, I saw Crangles' grave and I tell you… I shed a tear or two… excuse me… I felt it very much, it touched me. It does, even now to talk about it. But eventually I got round and I got over it.

When I go back I can cope with it better, but I still feel it about him, it brings it all back to me. It makes me live it all over again, what we went through. Not only seeing Crangles, seeing Scott and Corporal Close who later ended up as a sergeant and all those men who were killed. It all comes back to you, but you can't help feeling it, it's just there with you and I think you'll go to the grave with it. It's something you'll remember all your life.

I would like to be remembered by my family as someone who had a great love for them. I had an experience where I was converted fifty years ago, I trusted The Lord and my whole attitude to life has changed. I don't like war any more, although I've taken part in and speak of it, war is a horrible thing. It's horrible, to look and see your mates churned to bits, killed, lying wounded. Those images never

leave you all your life. I have a brighter outlook on life for I felt that I fought for something that I didn't want to see my grandchildren go through. I would never like to see them go through what I had to go through myself. Since the war ended I've had a good life. I carried on serving in the Reserve Forces and the Territorials and the Ulster Defence Regiment and places like that and my life was in the forces. I've led a very happy life. I've had a good wife, two good children, several good grandchildren and great grandchildren so I've had a lot in life to live for, so when my time comes to go, I hope I go out happy with very sweet memories.'

2023, Belfast
The Author

I unfortunately never had the opportunity to interview the men you have read about. When they were with us I, to my shame, was one of those who knew nothing of their deeds and their role in Operation Overlord and the liberation of Europe. I am, as we all should be, eternally grateful to film maker Brian Henry Martin to have had the foresight and ability to track down and win the confidence of these men and to break down the veterans' code of silence. I am doubly grateful that Brian chose to share the recordings he made with me, the broadcast footage and the many hours of unused material where the dark secrets are hidden. I had the pleasure of meeting one Royal Ulster Rifles veteran, George Horner of Carrickfergus who is in his 97th year. His memory of the horrors experienced in 1944 had understandably dimmed. George recounted one incident however which remained with him.

George HORNER:
'I remember one village, I can't remember the name of it, we were pinned down. I called up for tanks, heavy guns.

There was a sort of a shop on a corner and there was heavy fire coming from it so I attracted a tank and they blew it up. When we got up [to the shop] it was the only time I cried, there was three children… I heard afterwards it was an organisation called the Hitler Youth Movement and that they were part of it. It didn't help me any. That was the only time I shed a tear, you know. I thought, is this what it's come to.'

George's account cannot be verified, he cannot recall the name of the village or the date of the incident and indeed he could be recalling a number of incidents in those few short lines. His final memory is one of horror.

Of the eight men interviewed, I did however have the honour to meet one of them, Bill McConnell. In 2018 I had been working as an Ambulance Driver in Belfast. Late one evening I was tasked to transfer a patient who was being discharged following treatment from a Belfast hospital to his home in North Belfast. My colleague and I collected the patient and transferred him into the ambulance. As I was the driver I wasn't privy to the details of the patient who had been secured in the rear of the ambulance. On arriving at the destination address we transferred the patient from the trolley to a wheelchair and brought him into his house. I helped move him into his living room and made him comfortable in his favourite armchair. It was then, when he was settled and I looked up around the room that I realised who this man was. The room was dimly let and as my eyes adjusted to the light I could see that the walls were adorned with military memorabilia, group photographs, badges and medals. My gaze fell upon the wall opposite on a framed banner depicting the mythological image of Bellrophon, the original airborne warrior riding astride the divine winged stallion Pegasus depicted in light blue on a claret red background, the famous 'Pegasus Flash' of the Airborne Forces. At that moment I realised who this man was. I turned to him in his home with his

daughter Vivienne looking on and reached out my hand, I looked him in the eye and said, "You fought on D-Day." He immediately sat up straight, as if injected with some life-giving drug, and with a glint in his eye and a wide smile he reached out and shook my hand in a firm grip and said,

"I did son, I fought on D-Day."

Afterword

An Interview with Brian Henry Martin
Director, DoubleBand Films, Belfast

'We Fought on D-Day' began in 2003, I was working at DoubleBand Films making an archive series for BBC Northern Ireland called 'Super 8 Stories'. I was always a history buff and obsessed with the Second World War, this was part of my whole passion and interest coming into television. At the time, the big film landmark in terms of D-Day was 'Saving Private Ryan' which was released in 1998 and was shot in Ireland on the coast of Wexford. Director Stephen Spielberg made the landing at Omaha Beach so visceral and experiential that it put D-Day firmly back in people's imagination again. That was the sea landing, then the Spielberg produced television drama 'Band of Brothers' came after that, and you had the airborne story with the United States 101st Airborne Division. So, film and television all of a sudden were telling the definitive story of the D-Day landings. The power of film and television to define a story is immense. If we look at 'Titanic' for example, there was little mention of Titanic in this city before 1997, James Cameron's movie came out and became a billion-dollar box office hit, the most successful film of all time and now we have redefined the whole city, a quarter of the City of Belfast is named after the Titanic.

So that was the beginning, I can't pinpoint it exactly, but all of our documentaries start with a key question and in this case

the question was 'What did WE do on D-Day?' Surely, we must have done something, surely there must have been people from here (Northern Ireland) who fought on D-Day? It began like that because D-Day had become an American story not only because of Stephen Spielberg but also because of Stephen Ambrose the author who wrote a series of books from which 'Band of Brothers' was based. In popular culture D-Day had become a completely American conflict, I thought this can't be right and that was a thread that we started to pull. As the 60th anniversary of D-Day approached, there felt like there was a hidden story that needed to be told. I visited the Royal Ulster Rifles Museum and met Captain Jacky Knox and discovered that two battalions of the Ulster Rifles had fought on D-Day, an airborne battalion and a seaborne battalion, I thought it was incredible that I didn't know this. I then began to think of 'Band of Brothers' and who the local band of brothers could be who could tell this story. I began to piece together the soldiers who were still here, a cast of around eight to ten men, our band of brothers — to allow me to drill into their stories. With the help of the Ulster Rifles museum, I got a list of names of the remaining veterans, and I started to work my way through that list and that's how I found these men.

There were two important things which I set out from the beginning. The first was that the narrative of the documentary was always going to be from the bottom up. I did not want generals or majors, I wanted to tell the ordinary soldier's story. I wanted the history to be from the bottom up. At the time I was influenced by an amazing series from the BBC called 'The People's Century' which looked at every decade of the Twentieth Century but told the story from the perspective of the ordinary people, the working class and what they knew at the time, not what we know now. This was visualised in the film with Hamilton Lawrence, he recounted General Montgomery on the eve of D-Day standing on a Jeep and addressing the Ulstermen and Hamilton can be seen in a photograph of the event, and there he is, standing at the feet

of Montgomery. That photograph symbolised so much for me because I wasn't making a film about Montgomery, I was making a film about the men at Monty's feet. So firstly, I wanted to just have ordinary soldiers who haven't spoken about this in any depth before and secondly let's have them only speak about what they knew at that time, not what they had learnt afterwards. What they experienced at the actual time of the Normandy landings.

The title of the documentary was so important — 'We Fought On D-Day' was in effect a mission statement, the 'We' was a collective; 'We' for everybody here, all of Northern Ireland. It was 'We' fought on D-Day and that was very much an underlined 'We' because we had learnt so much about Omaha beach and what the Americans had done that we had completely forgotten about Sword Beach and what the British soldiers and British Airborne divisions had achieved. The idea was to have eight men, four who landed by sea and four who landed by air and to cut between the experiences of both. Very quickly I realised that the story would be about what happened after D-Day. I had to set out a time period for the film, how far back and how far forward to go with the story, for me the time period was from D-Day minus 2 to the liberation of Caen. The landing on the beach was only the beginning and I certainly didn't realise that it took five weeks for them to liberate Caen and suffer many casualties along the way. That came as a surprise to me, so I realised that the real story happened after they landed.

I went to visit the key characters, Bill McConnell, Richard Keegan, Stanley Burrows, and Jimmy Bowden who all told a different story, and then it was about adding voices to them. They were all very receptive to the idea but the biggest challenge for me was to get them to talk honestly about their thoughts and emotions. How did you feel? What did you think? In the glider about to land or in the landing craft before the doors open, how did you feel? What did you think? This is very difficult for trained soldiers because they don't think and they don't feel at those moments, they are trained to get on with it, not to stop and think

and not to stop and feel an emotion. They don't let their emotions or feelings take over what they must do. The biggest challenge for me was to bring them back to that moment and to pause them at every second. I only wanted them to tell me what they knew at the time, not what books they had read afterwards or what films they had seen.

The other challenge was what I called 'The code of war'. For a lot of those men their fathers had fought in the Great War and when they came home, they did not speak about what had happened on the battlefield. If they did speak, they talked to a fellow soldier who had also fought but they didn't tell their families. It didn't become a story that they told around the dinner table, and they certainly didn't have idle chat about it. There was a code, 'What happens on the battlefield stays on the battlefield and we don't reveal'. This was another challenge, I wanted to unlock that code and I wanted them to really speak openly about that experience and tell us about things that they felt, things that they saw, and the people who were sadly killed. Those were difficult things for soldiers to talk about. These men, well they were boys, they were teenagers at the time and when I met them they were in their eighties and I think there is a sweet spot there where they have lived a life and left this experience behind but the ghosts of the experiences come back and I met them at a moment where it felt like the right time to speak about it. They had nothing to lose, so why not speak about it? But that took a bit of persuasion. I wasn't doing that for shock or titillation or trivialisation, I just honestly wanted it to be real.

The documentary film, 'We Fought on D-Day' begins with Bill McConnell at Longueval at a service on the 6th of June and he said the words 'We will remember them,' but the truth is we haven't remembered them. We just haven't remembered them, and I felt that then. When Bill said those words, I thought to myself, 'You have remembered them Bill, but we have not.' That was wrong and we need to remember them, these were the men who lived, let

alone the men who had died. I felt ashamed of that and that was again part of the mission statement of the film, let's let these men speak, let's let them tell the story. It was not set out to be a military history with facts and figures, I set out to get under the experiences of these men and into the emotion. The film soundtrack was really key, an amazing graphic designer called Glen Marshall made the soundtrack for the documentary. It is really visceral and emotional, and it sets the tone for the whole film and created an audio bedrock to allow the men to speak. It lets the viewer know that this is not a military history but an experiential journey with these eight men for five weeks.

I went to see the men two or three times at home before we did any filming, just chatting but mainly just listening, I wanted them to feel comfortable so that when we came to the interview the camera would just disappear and they would forget that the camera was there, and they would just talk to me. Stanley and Bill were the two key characters in this for me, I got to know them very well and really respected both of them, they were so humble and unassuming about their whole actions that I was amazed. They were small men in stature, but they were giants. They just embraced the whole mission of the film and were incredibly open. For instance, when Stanley spoke about writing the letter home to his mother on the eve of D-Day, he was a boy basically writing his will and testament, it was such a powerful moment, no one was not going to be moved by that moment. Then Bill, who was a tough soldier, this was his first experience of conflict, but he went on to fight through Europe and in Palestine then Korea, he had this whole military career, but this was his first experience, as a teenager. But there was a moment where Bill spoke about coming under German shelling and he wanted his mother. He wanted his mammy! That is an incredible admission, what soldier would admit that, and he said, 'I'm not ashamed to admit it'. You realise that he too was just a boy, you have an old man in front of you, but he is speaking the words of a boy. That's incredibly powerful, those

little moments when they really opened up and let us in to what they were thinking at that moment. That's when I knew that these interviews had a real emotional power.

Both Stanley and Bill had these tragic experiences where friends of theirs had been killed. Bill told the story of Bobby Stevenson, a heartbreaking story where his friend was blown to pieces in front of him and because there was no officer present, he was recorded as missing. He's on the missing memorial and you could feel Bill's pain over that. Bill was so dignified when he went to the cemeteries, and he talked about seeing the young faces on the graves. Stanley talked about his best friend Hugh Crangles being killed and being haunted by this for sixty years until he went back and saw the beautifully preserved headstone and told us that he wept at the grave. I was really moved by that, and it reminds you what those cemeteries in faraway France are really for.

It was a very powerful thing to go to the village of Longueval and to see the Mayor of the town and the French people come out and pay their respects to these Ulster men who had liberated them and yet back here in Northern Ireland we had no knowledge of this and had completely forgotten, yet in Normandy here is this village where the people are incredibly grateful for what We had done. That felt like a really important thing to acknowledge.

You learn so much along the way, that the plan was to land on Sword Beach and cycle to Caen. They explained that they were landing in eight feet of water, under fire, full pack, gun, and they'd to carry a bicycle! Then there were the key locations like the battle for Cambes Wood, Richard Keegan set that up so eerily when he said, 'Will you come into my parlour said the spider to the fly.' It was so dramatic when you realise that this was when they were first going to encounter war. They thought it was going to be easy. They survived the beach head, or they had safely landed but then they encountered war, real war. Sam Lowry's description is so powerful when he said, 'War is grotesque, I can't describe the horrors of war... the physical damage, the mental damage' The

fact that he couldn't describe it made it even more powerful. The important thing for me was just to sit with someone like Sam for a moment, just to linger with that thought and have him explain to you that he can't describe it. It's more powerful than him trying to describe it.

We talked about how they felt about taking part in such a big military operation, the greatest landing in the history of warfare and also about how they would like to be remembered. They were all so humble about it. Richard said, 'They were all heroes, everyone who took part is a hero' and that's how I felt about it, but they said it, they were all heroes. These were ordinary fellows with ordinary jobs from ordinary backgrounds, they had never been on a boat before, they had never been in the air before, they certainly had never been to France before, it's important to go back and just register all of that because it seems so obvious.

Of course, I regret that we didn't do more filming with all of them. I wish we had have filmed them at home and I wish I had have filmed them all in France and I wish I had have filmed two or three interviews with all of them. The other regret I have is that we didn't just continue with the interviews and that I didn't just interview them about their entire war experiences, they had taken part in Operation Market Garden, they had taken part in crossing the Rhine, they had entered Germany then they went to Palestine and then some of them went to Korea. Marty Vance was a prisoner of war in Korea for a couple of years, so they had incredible experiences, and we were only touching on their first experience of war.

Before the documentary was broadcast on BBC Northern Ireland for the 60th anniversary of D-Day we had a screening at BBC Broadcasting House in Belfast and the eight men all came. They all met each other, some of them didn't know each other because they were from different battalions, they all came together, and they watched the film, and their families were there. That was a really powerful moment, and they were all recognised at that

moment for what they had done, and they were all thanked. For me that was a really powerful event where it felt like what they had fought for and what they had done had been remembered and they had been publicly thanked for what they had done.

The production had a great team, spearheaded by producer Dermot Lavery with camera David Barker, sound David Kilpatrick and editor David Gray. None of us will forget the experience of making 'We Fought on D-Day'.

Acknowledgements

I would like to thank a number of individuals for their valuable assistance in helping me create this work, all assistance provided to me has been very much appreciated. For access to the source material, original documentary research and for a unique form of quiet encouragement I wish to thank Dermot Lavery, Michael Hewitt, and Brian Henry Martin of DoubleBand Films in Belfast. Without their professional foresight over 20 years ago the original interviews with the men you have read about would not have been made and their remarkable accounts of June 1944 would now be lost forever. I am honoured to be able to use the same title for this book as it was used in their original film documentary.

My personal connection with DoubleBand extends back now over twelve years from when I contributed to the film documentary 'The Man Who Shot The Great War', incidentally also the title of what was to become my first book. This is now my third, each linked to the others with the common denominator being, DoubleBand Films. To make terrific documentary films is one thing, but to allow someone the ability to perhaps now call himself an author is something else. Thank you.

To Gavin Glass, Curator of the Royal Ulster Rifles Museum in Bedford Street in Belfast I would like to thank for facilitating access to the archives of the 1st and 2nd Battalions of the Royal Ulster Rifles held under his charge, and for drawing upon his knowledge of the Regiment.

I am indebted to the staff and Council of the Northern

Ireland War Memorial (NIWM) for their assistance in making the publication of this book a reality, thus helping to preserve the remembrance of those named within its cover. In particular I would like to thank the NIWM Council Chair, Colonel Don Bigger for his assistance both in Belfast and on the ground in Normandy, France.

A number of individuals assisted me with their own specific expertise, in particular I would like to mention Michael Jackson for giving up his valuable time and in sharing his knowledge of the workings of the National Archives. Tony Crawford for his technical knowledge and expertise. Tom McCarthy for his kind permission in using extracts from his book 'True Loyals' relating to the sinking of the SS *Sambut*. Paul Woodadge for his assistance with printing important extracts from the diary of his family member, the late Captain Cyril Rand. To Ben Mayne for sharing his knowledge of the East Riding Yeomanry and their part in the actions at Cambes en Plain in June 1944. To Stephen Carr for his permission to publish extracts from the diary of his grandfather, Joseph Peiestley who served with the East Riding Yeomanry.

I regret that with the passing of 20 years since the making of the DoubleBand Film documentary 'We Fought on D-Day' it has not been possible for me to track down the families of the men originally interviewed. I would, however like to thank Vivienne Bowman, Colin Burrows, Jamie Vance, Anne Greenlees, James Brudenell and Clare Davidson for their assistance and support. To Catherine Champion for information relating to her father Colonel Robin Charley.

In particular I would like to thank Warren Lyons for his help with facilitating contact with Doreen Fuller and to the extended Fuller/Whitehorn family for their support with this project.

I would like once again to thank Malcolm Johnston, Jacky Hawkes, and all at Colourpoint Books/Blackstaff Press for their assistance in producing this publication.

To Patricia Fawcett, for proofreading and support.

Finally, thanks to my wife Kim and daughters Kathryn and Lauren for support and patience.